THE MOSSER MASSACRE

The Southwest's Greatest Manhunt

GLENN SHIRLEY

EAKIN PRESS ⬥ Fort Worth, Texas
www.EakinPress.com

Revised edition of BORN TO KILL

Copyright © 2001
By Glenn Shirley
Published By Eakin Press
An Imprint of Wild Horse Media Group
P.O. Box 331779
Fort Worth, Texas 76163
1-817-344-7036
www.EakinPress.com
ALL RIGHTS RESERVED
1 2 3 4 5 6 7 8 9
ISBN-13: 978-1-940130-18-7

CONTENTS

William Edward (Billy) Cook, Jr.—gun-crazy killer with the "hard luck" hands.

PREFACE

On December 30, 1950, Carl and Thelma Mosser, of Atwood, Illinois, were happily en route to Albuquerque, New Mexico, with their three children—Ronald, six; Gary, five; and Pamela, three—for a family reunion.

While traveling U.S. Highway 66 near Luther, Oklahoma, they spotted a youth waving a signal of distress. The Mossers, kind-hearted people, stopped to lend assistance.

That was the beginning of an ordeal of terror for the Mossers—nightmarish days spent under the youth's gun while they drove aimlessly through Oklahoma, Texas, Arkansas, and Missouri.

Their grimy, blood-stained Chevrolet sedan, found mired in a roadside ditch two miles northwest of Tulsa the morning of January 3, 1951, set off the Southwest's greatest manhunt. In the twelve days that followed, some 2,000 peace officers sought the gun-crazy terrorist in fourteen states and Mexico. At the same time, hundreds of others—officials and private citizens—in planes, helicopters, automobiles, on horseback and afoot, searched mountain passes, canyons, and river beds for the victims of his orgy of violence.

This is the story of droopy-eyed William Edward "Billy" Cook, Jr., with the "hard luck" hands, who triggered half a dozen murders and kidnapped as many other victims in his flight to Baja California and the Pacific. "I'm going to live by the gun, and roam," was his credo. He was one of America's most elusive and homicidal psychopaths.

I was a police captain in Oklahoma during Cook's heinous escapades. My account is based on personal knowledge of the chase; contemporary reports; numerous interviews with local, state, and federal officers who participated; and the statements of witnesses and persons who knew Cook before he became the nation's most wanted fugitive.

Glenn Shirley
Stillwater, Oklahoma

CHAPTER 1

"I'M GONNA MAKE SOME BIG DOUGH, BABY"

He was a stocky youth, with wavy, dark brown hair, a wide, rather even nose, thick, sensual lips, and an olive-skinned face. He blushed easily. Well groomed, he was almost handsome, except for a peculiar, droopy-eyed expression that made him appear sullen. He didn't smoke or drink. He rarely touched even a glass of beer, and refused the shot of rum offered him by the pretty little night dancer in Juarez.

He had checked in at an El Paso hotel the evening of December 27, 1950, and decided to cross the border into Mexico to have some fun. He had run into the girl in a round of backstreet clip joints where strip-teasers and the bawdy jokes of the master of ceremonies were the principal features. They had danced and kissed briefly. He had offered to get her a passport and take her home with him to Missouri; she had refused.

When he tried to fondle her, she pushed him away and laughed. "You're just homesick, Billy," she said. "You *need* a drink."

"No," he replied. "I spent Christmas in a Blythe, California, bar. I got different plans for New Year's."

So she drank her portion ceremoniously, holding her glass in both hands. "To you and Missouri, then, Billy—and a happy New Year."

The youth swallowed hard. He turned to the window, gazing over the tops of low brown-stucco buildings sprawled in the moonlight, as if completely oblivious of the girl at the table and the samba dancers who cavorted crazily before them. With his droopy right eye half closed, he grew more sullen as the seconds ticked on.

He sat for a long minute, brooding. When he turned back to the girl, his thick neck had reddened, and he shook his head slowly back and forth, as if almost angry.

"Okay, baby." He removed a brown leather windbreaker from the back of his chair and slipped into it. "I'll see you when I get back from Missouri," he said over his shoulder. "It won't be long. I'm gonna make some big dough, maybe $18,000—then *I'm comin' back!*" He shoved his way through the dancers and went down into the street.

The throbbing beat of the rumba, samba, conga, bolero, and other exotic rhythms surrounded him—maddened him. Instinctively, he lifted a hand to his face. One finger touched the drooping eye.

This is why she wouldn't let me make love to her—why she wouldn't go with me to Missouri, he thought.

Always that eye had been his handicap—the result of an operation in infancy that made the lid set nearly halfway across the ball so that he was unable to close it completely. It had hurt him with women. It had kept him from obtaining a decent job. He had learned, when very young, how repulsive it was to people.

He turned into Stanton Avenue and walked toward the International Bridge and El Paso. Through the screen of garish neons twinkled the necklace of lights that outlined the sluggish Rio Grande, barely knee-deep to the urchins who had stood in water and clamored for his pennies when he had crossed that afternoon.

The wind blew colder, and he shivered beneath the short jacket. The revelry from the nightclubs was lost behind. Somewhere along the street a clock struck 1:00 as the lonely, bitter youth checked into his hotel.

A few hours later, he was hitchhiking east on U.S. Highway 180. In one hand he carried a small brown duffel bag, in the right pocket of his jacket was a new .32 Colt's semi-automatic pistol, and in his mind was the plan he had worked out a few weeks earlier.

It was Friday morning, December 28, 1950. Within seven days he would become the leading topic of radio dispatches, while the nation's newspapers splashed his name in big, scary headlines comparing him with such criminal legends as Clyde Barrow, Pretty Boy Floyd, and John Dillinger.

CHAPTER 2
"THAT DROOPY EYE—IT GIVES YOU THE CREEPS"

He was alone for a day and then fate threw him together with an auto mechanic named Lee Burd Archer. Archer, a tall, thin man, gray-haired and stooped by his fifty-eight years, left his home at Tahoka, Texas, on the night of December 28 to drive to Oklahoma City to visit friends.

He sped the short distance north on Highway 87 to Lubbock in his sleek black Buick convertible, and turned east on U.S. 82. He had made the trip before, and remembering the nearly three hundred miles of monotonous land of short grass and high plains sprawling eastward from the Cap Rock country, he searched for companionship.

In the early morning hours of December 29, as he pulled away from a service station east of Lubbock, he spotted a stocky, hatless youth in a fur-collared windbreaker, giving him the hitcher's thumb signal.

Archer braked to a stop.

"How far you going, son?"

"Joplin, Missouri."

Archer looked him over, saw that he carried a small brown duffel bag, and aside from a drooping right eyelid that stamped a perpetual leer on his features, he appeared to be just one of the many hitchhikers to be found at that time of year on any main highway. "Well, I can take you part way. Hop in."

Archer made small talk as he drove on. "I'm off for the holidays. Going to Oklahoma City. . . Nice weather, wasn't for the cold wind. No telling what that wind will fetch up by New Year's."

Busy driving, he failed to notice that the youth kept his right hand in his jacket pocket. "Going to Joplin, eh? Fine town. I've been there. Before the war, though. Don't reckon it's the same place now. Where you been, son?"

The youth mentioned Mexico, but his voice was so low it was barely audible. He was studying Archer closely. He volunteered no further information about himself; Archer didn't press the conversation.

At Benjamin, Texas, they stopped at an all-night restaurant for pie and coffee. Then they sped on through the night in silence. The droopy-eyed youth dozed most of the time, and when, after crossing Red River into Oklahoma shortly before daybreak, Archer tried to start another conversation, he didn't answer.

At Chickasha, they stopped for breakfast. The youth said he wasn't hungry and would wait outside. As Archer started to enter the roadside cafe, he noticed the youth hanging back near the car. On the excuse that he had forgotten something, he returned to the convertible. For a moment he searched in the glove compartment, then locked the car doors before entering the diner.

Afterwards, as their ride continued northeastward, Archer glanced at the youth narrowly. He seemed like a nice guy, clean and neat. For the first time he was smiling. It was a funny smile, though, like a kid caught stealing something. It gave Archer an odd feeling, and he decided to get rid of him as soon as he reached Oklahoma City. Entering the outskirts, he turned into a shortcut on Southwest 29th Street, which would take him to the downtown business section within a few minutes.

Obviously the youth had anticipated his move. Archer caught a quick movement from the corner of his eye. He looked around into the muzzle of a nickel-plated automatic.

The youth sat against the back of the seat as if braced for a sudden stop. His face was contemptuous and his dark eyes gleamed dangerously. The right eye was a narrow slit in its half-closed lid. "Keep driving, mister. I'm engineering this trip from here. We ain't stoppin' nowhere till I say so."

"What's the matter, son?" Archer demanded, as calmly as possible. "Have you gone nuts?"

The leer enveloped the youth's features. "I'll shoot if you stop this car. I'll shoot if you call out. You better do what I say." He tilted the automatic until the muzzle pointed straight at Archer's head. His right eye was almost closed.

"If you want my car, take it," Archer said.

"And let you go squealin' to the cops?"

"You got no use for me."

"Don't give me any lip. Do what I say!"

With the automatic aimed at his head, Archer drove through Oklahoma City. A few miles north, near Edmond, he picked another shortcut, which he told the youth would take them onto U.S. Highway 66 leading to Tulsa and Joplin. Though he had been over the course before, Archer missed a turn, and after driving for twenty minutes through unfamiliar country, he decided to go back.

"No," the youth ordered. "Stop the car."

The Buick spewed up a cloud of red dust as it skidded to a halt.

Archer felt the muzzle of the shiny automatic gouge his ribs.

"All right, mister. Get out."

Archer obeyed. The youth stepped out close behind him, calmly rifled his pockets and removed his wallet. Archer knew it contained $85. He had counted his money when he paid his breakfast at Chickasha. Then the youth ordered him to the back of the car and told him to open the trunk compartment.

Archer walked to the rear of the convertible, his face immobile. He opened the compartment. Inside lay the spare tire, a litter of old road maps, tire chains, and tools. He knew what the youth had in mind. "There isn't room in there," he said.

The youth cursed and shoved him against the lid. "Get in!"

Again Archer pleaded with him. "Give me a break and let me go."

"Get in, I said."

"You've got my money, and you can have the car."

"Goddamnit, shut up—or I'll kill you now!" The youth jabbed him hard with the automatic.

Archer climbed in, curling himself on the trunk floor. The lid was slammed down. He heard the gunman walk to the driver's side. The motor roared to life, gears clashed in reverse as the car turned around, then went rocking away at high speed over the rough country road.

Inside the trunk, Archer took the worst jolting ride of his life. The car went fast, then very slow. The gears kept clashing, and Archer realized the youth was unfamiliar with its operation. He groped among the tools, found a screwdriver, and went to work on the compartment lock. Finally, he jimmied it open.

When the car labored on a hill and slowed again, he decided to take a chance. Throwing open the lid, he jumped. He hit the road rolling and pawing up dirt and gravel. The youth heard the trunk fly open. Through the rear-view mirror he saw Archer leap. The car brakes squealed. He stepped out, waving the automatic.

"Come back, you sonovabitch, or I'll kill you!"

Archer scrambled to his feet and ran blindly for the brush. Every step he took he expected a bullet to smash into his back. But, for some reason, the youth didn't fire.

Archer ran faster. He reached the brush and crashed into it, out of sight. Arms outflung, he lay on his face, motionless. His breath rattled in his throat and his heart banged inside his chest like a trip hammer. He waited, but the youth didn't follow. He heard the gears clash again. The Buick roared away in a cloud of dust.

Then Archer was on his feet, running again.

A few minutes later he reached the home of Fred McAlester. The farmer didn't have a phone, but offered to drive him to the nearest service station at Luther, where he called the Oklahoma County sheriff's office.

Meanwhile, the young gunman, still experiencing difficulty with Archer's automobile, reached Highway 66 and turned eastward. On a curve near Luther, the car stalled and died. He was unable to start it again.

He saw a car approaching from the east—a blue Chevrolet sedan driven by 33-year-old Carl Mosser of Atwood, Illinois. With him were his wife, Thelma, and their three children—Ronald Dean, 7, Gary Carl, 5, and Pamela Sue, 3. They were en route to Albuquerque, New Mexico, to visit Mosser's twin brother, Chris— an Air Force lieutenant attached to a military police unit at Sandia Base. Lieutenant Mosser had been recalled to active duty a few months earlier, and the journey was twofold—a reunion at New Year's and a celebration for Ronald Dean's eighth birthday.

"Take U.S. 66 all the way," Chris had advised when Carl called long-distance to ask the best possible route.

Carl and Thelma Mosser and their three children posed for this backyard shot at their Illinois home just before their fatal car trip to New Mexico.

It was the family's first big trip away from home, and the back seat was piled high with extra clothing, traveling gear, and blankets so the children could nap while the parents took turns driving.

The youth stepped from the Buick stalled on the curve and waved the signal of distress. The Mossers, kind-hearted farm people and desirous of doing a neighborly act, stopped to lend assistance.

Kermit Mackey, a resident of the Luther community, rounded the curve behind them. He saw the black convertible and the blue Chevrolet on opposite sides of the highway. "The two cars were facing each other," he recalled afterward, "about a hundred yards apart. The car headed east had Texas plates. Its driver ran across the road. His hands were in the side pockets of his jacket, and he kept his head down as I passed. I looked back and saw him getting in the other car."

Mackey returned from town a few minutes later and found the Buick still sitting halfway on the slab, so when he reached home, he notified the State Highway Patrol.

His call was received at 11:30 A.M., just after Archer had reported his experiences at the hand of the gunman to the Oklahoma County sheriff's office. Trooper Luzon Smith of the Highway Patrol drove to the scene. The car had lost its oil. The bearings were burned out. The motor and water were still hot.

The trooper had the car towed to a garage in Luther. By noon, Archer had reclaimed it.

Oklahoma County's chief criminal investigator, Y.V. Burks, and Deputy Don Stone arrived from Oklahoma City to complete the investigation. So far as they were concerned, it was a quick recovery of a stolen automobile. The next step was to identify the gunman and put out a routine alarm for him.

Mackey furnished a description. "He was dark-haired, five feet seven inches tall and weighed about 155 pounds. He was wearing gray trousers, a brown leather jacket and a red shirt. He was bare-headed."

The search for fingerprints yielded nothing. But the officers found the brown duffel bag the gunman had left in the car. The contents looked promising. There were several T-shirts bearing the laundry mark initials "W. E. C.," a box which had contained a new .32 Colt's automatic, a cleaning brush for the pistol, and a box containing thirty-six rounds of .32-caliber ammunition.

The absence of fourteen cartridges suggested that the gunman had escaped with at least fourteen shots for his weapon.

There was a receipt for the purchase of the pistol from an El Paso store, showing the serial number of the weapon and made out to "W. E. Cook, St. Louis."

There were probably a thousand W. E. Cooks in the country, and this was a very general lead—even if it was the gunman's right name. But the bag held one more clue, something more definite. It was a photograph of three children—two boys and a girl—in a frame bearing the name of a studio at Kirksville, Missouri.

The deputies returned to Oklahoma City and began the task of tracing the picture's owner. Bob Turner, Oklahoma County's long-time, crime-busting sheriff, wrote a letter to Kirksville. Burks and Stone cancelled the stolen report on Archer's car and broadcast the description of the gunman supplied by Mackey.

"He's ugly through and through," Archer added. "I'd know him anywhere—even across the street from me on a dark night. That droopy eye of his—it gives you the creeps."

The youth had commandeered the best possible vehicle in which to escape. The Mosser sedan was a widely used make of unobtrusive color and along U.S. 66—the "Main Street of America" where traffic roared along day and night—was totally inconspicuous. Numbering himself among its passengers—a man, his wife, and three children—he was comparatively safe from suspicion.

Yet one more point was checked in the route taken by the family. Shortly before noon, Claud Seymour, an agent for the State Crime Bureau who was parked at the junction of U.S. 66 and 77, saw the car going west toward Edmond.

"I happen to remember the dark blue Chevrolet because it was in a long line of traffic that I was checking closely for the Buick stolen in the hijacking," Seymour reported.

"It was a 1949 model, with Illinois plates, a sun visor and red attachments on the wind wings. Two men were in the front seat, a woman and children in the back. The man beside the driver was bare-headed and wore a jacket with a fur collar. I thought it unusual that he should be dressed in such a heavy garment while the others all wore light clothing. Then the line passed."

At that time the description of the gunman and the car he had entered had not been broadcast.

Seymour did not realize that he was the last witness to the beginning of the most vicious terror-ride in the annals of crime.

CHAPTER 3

"HE'S GOING TO KILL MY WIFE AND CHILDREN"

There was a heartbreaking hope of rescue for the family when at 7 P.M. their blue Chevrolet stopped on the outskirts of Wichita Falls, Texas—later that same day—just south of Red River, where early that morning, the gunman and his first victim had crossed into Oklahoma.

The car pulled up to a little combination service station and grocery store called Roy's Station.

Inside, E. O. Cornwell, the elderly, one-legged attendant, shifted the crutch under his left shoulder and whistled softly to himself as he industriously sliced a piece of ham for Claude Skinner, a forty-year-old Wichita Falls pipeline worker. Tossing the cut on the scales, Cornwell squinted through his bifocals to check the weight, and was about to tear a sheet of wrapping paper when he saw the car with two men in front and a woman and children in the back seat pull up at the gasoline pump.

"Let me catch them folks," he said to Skinner. "It'll only take a minute."

Skinner was in no hurry. He moved toward the end of the counter, checking other meats in the glass case as Cornwell removed his white apron and hobbled outside.

"Yes, sir! Fill 'er up?" asked Cornwell.

The stocky youth who slumped beside the driver nodded, and Cornwell hurried to the rear of the vehicle. As he pumped gasoline into the tank, he noticed that the children in the back seat were restless. They were wrapped in blankets and the woman was trying to quiet them.

"Okay, mister," Cornwell called cheerily. The driver paid him for the gasoline and asked if he had some lunch meat.

"No time for that!" The youth beside him was sitting erect.

The driver insisted. "The children are hungry."

"If you want some lunch meat," said Cornwell, "you'll have to come inside and get it."

The driver stepped from the car, and the youth followed immediately. His right hand was in his jacket pocket. He was about twenty-four, Cornwell guessed. He was hatless, and the attendant observed that his hair was dark brown and wavy. The other man was eight or ten years older, slender and lean-featured, with light hair, cut crew style. He seemed worried about the woman and children.

Cornwell went back inside, and the two men followed. As they entered the store, the youth said something to the older man in a low voice.

Then, suddenly, the man in front flung himself at his companion and grabbed him.

The older man pinioned his arms. "For God's sake, help me!" he pleaded with Cornwell. "He's been with us all day—he's got a gun and he's going to kill my wife and children!"

Cornwell was bewildered. "If he's got a gun, get him out of here," he replied. "I don't want any shooting in my store."

The youth struggled to free himself, and the pair tottered about the room like drunken dancers while the older man kept shouting, "He's going to kill me—he's going to kill all of us!"

From the car outside came the muffled crying of the children. The shouting and scuffling in the store had alarmed them.

Their outbursts seemed to lend the youth the strength he needed. Like a wolf shaking a dog off its back, he swung the older man around and slammed him against the wall, shattering a window.

Cornwell's temper flared. He hopped behind the counter, fumbled in a drawer, and whipped out a .44 Colt's "thumb-buster" revolver.

The crash against the window had loosened the older man's

-Photo by Wichita Falls Times

HE RAN 'EM OFF—O. E. Cornwell, 63-year-old one-legged operator of Roy's service station, west of Wichita Falls on the Iowa Park highway, is believed to have seen the kidnapped Carl Mosser family of Illinois Saturday night. Above, Cornwell tells Sheriff Hammett Vance of Wichita Falls that the two men scuffled in his store and one of them exclaimed "This man is trying to kill me!" Whereupon, Cornwell grip. But he was still able to hold the youth, who was trying to work his hand back into his jacket pocket.

Cornwell pointed his revolver at them and ordered the older man to let go. The man hesitated. Cornwell threatened to shoot him. He let go.

Then the youth was in command again. His hand was in his jacket pocket, and he ordered the older man back to the car.

"Hey," yelled Cornwell, "who's going to pay for this window?"

The men left without answering.

"Stop them!" he shouted to Skinner.

Skinner, who had been standing tense-faced and frozen, ran to the door. The youth was shoving the older man into the car. He was saying something, but Skinner couldn't understand him.

In the dim light from the gas pump, he glimpsed the woman's face through the rear glass, round-eyed, filled with terror. Then the car doors closed, and the Chevrolet sped away in the darkness.

Skinner's pickup was parked nearby. Cornwell was shouting for him to get the license number. And Skinner, wanting to help his elderly, one-legged friend if he could, leaped into his truck and tore off in pursuit.

He came up on the blue car as it turned west along the ten-mile stretch of highway toward Iowa Park. He picked up its license plate in his headlights, and was almost close enough to read the numerals when the youth in the leather jacket opened fire on him.

Two shots struck the gravel in front of the truck and ricocheted. Skinner slowed down, stopped, and turned back. He drove to the nearest telephone. The operator connected him with the home of Sheriff Hammett Vance of Wichita County. Vance, a tall, lean-faced Texan—still in his forties but with plenty of law enforcement experience—drove to Roy's Station to make an investigation.

Cornwell told his story. "I want them caught," he concluded. "Somebody's gonna pay for that window."

The Chevrolet, traveling fast, had reached Iowa Park by that time. Vance called the peace officer of the little Texas community of 2,000 and asked him to be on the lookout.

The sheriff found a gray felt hat in the driveway that Cornwell and Skinner hadn't seen before.

"Both men were bare-headed when they came in the store,"

Cornwell said. "It must have got kicked out when they went back to the car."

"Or thrown out on purpose," Skinner suggested. "The woman—I saw her face as they drove away. She was scared."

The hat was size seven, bearing a label of "The Famous Store, Decatur, Ill."

Skinner thought the car bore an Illinois plate. "I noticed how my lights flashed on it. It was silver color."

Decatur was twenty-four miles from Atwood, Illinois, home of the Mosser family. But at the moment the label held no significance to Sheriff Vance. He kept the hat as evidence in event the vehicle was apprehended, and again contacted the officer at Iowa Park to give him the additional license information.

"Get over here right away," the officer told him. "The car was here, all right. Four boys saw it—talked to one of the parties—and I think you should hear their story."

Half an hour later, Sheriff Vance was talking to teenagers Raymond Smith, Jackie Sampson, Olen Roberts, and Reuben Copeland.

According to young Smith, they had been walking through the park along Lafayette Street when the car stopped beside them. "The curly-haired passenger in the front seat cranked down his window and asked Jackie, 'How do we get out of here on a back road?' Jackie told him there was no other way, and he said, 'There is—I know there is!'

"While Jackie was talking, we looked in the car and saw a woman sitting on the floor with a blanket wrapped around her. Some kids were on the floor at her side. She kept shaking her head and pointing with her fingers, first to us, then to the man in front, as if trying to warn us about something. But, before we could do anything, the man beside the driver said, 'Okay, let's go,' and the Chevy drove off."

They had last seen it traveling west on Highway 27.

Sheriff Vance studied all this information. He had not heard of the hijacking in Oklahoma nor how the gunman had escaped in a blue Chevrolet bearing Illinois plates. There was nothing particularly sinister about the case initially, nothing to hint that this routine investigation would develop into a macabre mystery.

He sent a pickup order as far west as Amarillo, but the car was not intercepted.

CHAPTER 4

HOPE OF RESCUE FADES

The Chevrolet and its occupants were not seen again until Monday, January 1. At 4:30 P.M., on the day Carl Mosser had expected to be driving into his brother Chris' place at Albuquerque. Mrs. Rufus Smith—of Winthrop, Arkansas, a small community on Little River, deep in the southwestern corner of the state and miles east of the Oklahoma line—watched the man and the youth enter her combination grocery store and cafe.

Mrs. Sherman Tuttle, an employee, observed the woman and children in the car outside. She noted that the car bore an Illinois license, that the two boys were redheaded, and the baby girl was a curly blonde. The children were begging for water, and the mother had been crying.

The man took a stool at the counter and ordered seven ham sandwiches, then he had Mrs. Smith fill a quart fruit jar with water and a thermos bottle with coffee. He ordered a box of cough drops, six bottles of soda pop, two packs of Lucky Strike cigarettes, and a penny box of matches to take with him. The droopy-eyed youth waited silently near the doorway with one hand rammed in his jacket pocket. He kept peering out the window and appeared very sleepy.

While Mrs. Smith prepared the sandwiches, the man drank a cup of coffee. Mrs. Tuttle, who served him, remarked that she was formerly of Illinois, and asked: "What part of the state are you from?"

"Atwood—" The man choked out the word. He seemed to be wanting to tell her something, but the youth walked up as she began talking. He sat at the counter and kept watching outside with an animal-like vigilance the woman hadn't noticed before.

The man finished his coffee. When the sandwiches were ready, he paid the $3.38 check for the articles purchased. The youth prodded him back to the car, and they left, heading north on State Highway 41.

Tulsa, Oklahoma, a metropolitan area of over Oklahoma and famed as the "Oil Capital of the World," is approximately 250 miles from Winthrop.

At 8:30 A.M. the morning of January 2, Pete Essley, an Osage County rancher, was driving his ranch pickup when he saw the mud-spattered blue Chevrolet sedan mired in the soft shoulder of the bar ditch—just off lonely Osage Drive, two miles northwest of the oil capital city.

A youth stood in the roadway, unshaven and apparently nervous, his right hand in his jacket pocket. Essley locked both doors of his pickup before he stopped.

The youth asked if he could pull him out of the ditch.

Essley could see that the car was bogged to the axle. "My truck is too light for the job," he said.

"How far back to a place where I can get some help?" the youth asked.

Essley told him the Osage Hills shopping center was nearby. "If you want me to call somebody from there—"

"No," the youth said.

Essley drove on.

When Lloyd Edwards, an oil company employee, drove past fifteen minutes later, the youth waved him down and asked for a ride to the shopping center.

Edwards told him it was against company rules to give rides in a company car. "I have a car telephone. I'll call a wrecker."

"No!" the youth said sharply.

Edwards studied his plight a moment and finally consented to give him a lift. He dropped him at the Crawford drugstore in the shopping center, and saw him go inside.

The youth approached Charles Berkey, a clerk in the pharmacy, and he nervously fumbled a dollar bill and asked for change. "I want to call a cab."

Berkey gave him the change. He tried to call a taxi, but he wasn't familiar with Tulsa's dialing system. Berkey placed the call for him.

Taxi driver Willie Murphy tried to engage the youth in conversation as he drove him downtown. He wouldn't talk. But he couldn't keep still. He sat close to the door, squirming and fidgeting, fondling something in his jacket pocket and casting furtive glances at the passing traffic. His thick lips and droopy eye caused Murphy to think he might be Japanese.

He dropped the youth at a barbershop on the corner of Third Street and Cincinnati. The fare was sixty cents. The boy gave Murphy seventy-five cents and told him to keep the change.

Barber Tony Pagano trimmed his hair and shaved him. He noticed the muddy condition of his gray trousers and brown loafer shoes. Then the youth left the barbershop and disappeared.

The day passed. The cold drizzle that had set in during morning turned to intermittent rain and sleet. The blue Chevrolet remained in the ditch.

Because this section of Tulsa lies in Osage County, an Osage County deputy sheriff, Warren Smith, was notified of the abandoned car. Smith received the call at 10:45 P.M. Due to the inclement weather, he waited until the next morning, January 3, to investigate.

He jotted down the license number "Illinois 233-250," then opened the car door. A baby's shoe—a scuffed brown oxford—fell out in the mud. Smith stared.

A quick glance into the interior of the car showed him a bullet-punctured rear seat, stained and torn blankets, children's clothing smeared with blood, and pools of half-dried blood on the floor.

He stepped back to his cruiser and radioed Tulsa police headquarters.

CHAPTER 5

"SEEING THIS CAR MAKES YOU KNOW THEY ARE DEAD"

Within a few minutes the area was swarming with police detectives and sheriff officers. Deputy Smith and a posse began searching the surrounding, blackjack-covered hills and roadside ditches. Bruce Lovelace, chief criminal deputy of Tulsa County, and Police Technician Sam Shepherd examined the automobile.

There was a pathetic scattering of personal belongings which the family had brought on their cross-country trip, an empty quart fruit jar that had contained water, and a thermos bottle half-filled with coffee. There was a boy's baseball glove, a child's paint book, a doll, a toy doctor's kit, Hopalong Cassidy cowboy hats, and three wrappers and sticks from ice cream bars, as if three children had carelessly tossed them on the floor. A package of Lucky Strike cigarettes and some soft drink bottle caps lay in the front seat.

The ignition key was still in the car. In the glove compartment was a small box camera, a fresh roll of film, and a woman's purse. Besides the usual feminine articles, the purse contained a set of spare keys to the car, a pad of $200 in unused travelers checks, some family snapshots, and a driver's license in the name of Thelma Mosser, 29, Atwood, Illinois.

One of the snapshots showed a youthful, smiling couple with

Search scene northwest of Tulsa, Oklahoma, in Osage County, where the Mossers' mud-spattered blue Chevrolet sedan was found mired in the soft shoulder of a roadside ditch, January 2, 1951.

their arms around three youngsters—two boys and a curly-haired baby girl.

Piled in disarray on the back seat was a baby's dress, a pair of boy's jeans, an older boy's shirt, a man's jacket, and a woman's coat.

Lovelace picked up a blue baby blanket and pointed to a small hole in the center of it. The area around the hole was badly scorched. A gun, he reflected grimly, had been pressed against the cloth.

Other evidence of what had happened was a ripped pillowcase, knotted strips torn from a Turkish towel, seven brass shells which had been ejected by a .32 automatic pistol, and four bullet holes within an eight-inch area in the upper right of the seat cushion.

Beneath the bullet holes was a large pool of coagulated blood. On the armrest lay a short-billed green cap like the one worn by the youngest boy in the photograph. It, too, was splotched with blood.

Blood was everywhere. It had sprayed and splattered over the cushions, over the side upholstery, almost to the roof of the car, as if the victims had flailed about in agony.

With a penknife, Shepherd cut four spent bullets from the upholstery. He studied them a moment. They had been partially cleaned from passing through the fabric. But they still bore faint traces of gore. Clinging to one was a strand of blond hair.

A bullet hole in the front seat angled off as if the driver had been shot at the wheel.

"A whole family has been murdered! There's no question about it," Lovelace said. "But who did it? And why? And where are the bodies?"

Officials and volunteers scouring the area had found no blood trail, no footprints.

Detectives Jimmy Jackson and Ed Underhill discovered a spent slug several feet from the car. They believed the shots had been fired on the spot where the car was ditched.

Lovelace figured the bullet had fallen from a bloodstained blanket which had been removed from the vehicle. The blanket had been stuffed under the right rear wheel in an apparent effort to pull the car out of the mud.

Deputy Smith and a posse continued to search for the bodies, and the Chevrolet was towed to Tulsa police headquarters for an intensive laboratory examination.

A Tulsa police dispatcher sent a teletype to the Illinois state police at Springfield, and the word came back: "Tag registered to Carl Mosser, Atwood—no stolen report." Lovelace put through long-distance calls to authorities in the little village on the southern border of Piatt County, and to the sheriff's office at Monticello. Within an hour, he had the story of the family's departure at 2:20 P.M., Friday, December 29, for New Mexico. They had not arrived, and Carl's twin brother had called the Atwood home Monday night to learn what had caused the delay.

"There's a remote possibility the father turned on his family," Lovelace speculated.

Relatives said the idea was "fantastic."

Kenneth Bishop, a nephew and neighbor, described Carl as a good-natured fellow, always quiet and easy-going.

"He wasn't a war veteran. They took Chris but left Carl to run the farm. He never carried a gun—never owned any kind of firearm except a rifle, and it is still here.

"He just wasn't the kind of man to do that. He never showed any sign of insanity or cruelty. He was a good Joe."

In fact, there was nothing about Carl Mosser that was unusual. His name wasn't famous. During his thirty-three years, he hadn't done anything to make him particularly well-known. Few people outside the farming community in southern Piatt County knew him at all.

He had married Thelma Barcus, a girl living in Hammond, only a short distance from the farm where he was born. Together they began to build a future. Their first child was Ronald Dean, better known as "Ronnie." Gary Carl, another redhead, came along next. Then there was Pamela Sue, a little blond and the apple of her mother's eye.

Carl had rented a 160-acre farm and settled down in its neat white, seven-room frame house. He was a good farmer. His neighbors and businessmen in the nearby towns respected him. He was making a comfortable living for his family, even managing to save some money.

No, there wasn't much of the unusual about Carl Mosser.

"He and Thelma were just about the happiest couple you ever saw," Mrs. Helen Marshall, an aunt, said. "They've been married nearly ten years. Carl was devoted to his family, and close to his twin brother."

Chris and his wife, Ailene, and their two-year-old daughter, Linda Sue, had spent a leave in November visiting Carl and his family in Atwood.

"The trip to Albuquerque was in the form of a reunion and to celebrate Ronnie's birthday with a party in Uncle Chris' home," Mrs. Marshall added.

"That is the terrible part of it all. Tomorrow Ronnie would have been—I mean he will be—eight years old. I know nothing has happened to them."

A cousin, who worked in a bank at Hammond, told Lovelace, "Whatever happened, the motive must have been robbery. Carl had two hundred dollars cash besides the travelers' checks when he left Atwood. I sold him the checks and gave him the cash myself in new five- and ten-dollar bills. Somebody must have tried to stick him up and he took a swing at him. We Mossers have never liked anybody who tried to steal from us."

Lovelace obtained a description of the Mossers: Carl was five feet, four inches tall, with light brown hair and medium complexion, and weighed 150 pounds. Thelma was a bit taller, slender—a nice-looking woman.

Other members of both families—Leslie Barcus of Hammond, Mrs. Mosser's father; Clarence Day of Bement and Orin Dash of Decatur, Mosser's brothers-in-law; and Elmer Mosser, a nephew, also of Decatur—left for Tulsa immediately to assist in the search.

Chris Mosser, with his wife and daughter, Linda Sue—driving without stopping—arrived from Albuquerque.

"We started looking for them New Year's Day," Chris told police. "When they didn't arrive Tuesday, I called home. The folks told me they were on the way."

The tense-faced lieutenant brushed red eyes with his right arm. As he stood before his brother's blood-spattered car, he said softly, "Somebody's got to pay for this."

Chris was only a half-inch taller than his brother, and they weighed about two pounds of each other. He wasn't a large man, but the officers knew they had best get their hands on the murderer first.

"I've known Thelma since we were kids in grade school at Hammond," Ailene Mosser sobbed. She was an attractive brunette, three years older than Carl's wife. Her face was haggard with anxiety. She didn't expect to see the family alive again. "I know there isn't any hope. There can't be. I wish there could, but just seeing this car makes you know they are dead."

Little Linda Sue, too young to understand why she was in Tulsa, was asked by a reporter: "Who made your blue skirt and that skirt for your doll?"

"Aunt Thelma," the child said, proudly.

CHAPTER 6

AN UNEXPLAINED 2,400 MILES

Lieutenant Mosser, refusing to rest after his trip from Albuquerque, accompanied Deputy Smith to the spot where the car had been recovered. Fourteen highway patrolmen, led by Lieutenant Dave Faulkner commanding the Tulsa detachment, were assigned to the area, and a hundred other officers and citizens pressed a frantic but concentrated search for five bullet-torn, bound, and gagged bodies that were possibly lying somewhere in the rugged Osage Hills.

But local investigators were not convinced the family would be located so easily. The fact that the car had backed into the ditch, in an apparent attempt of the killer to turn around, indicated he had disposed of his victims earlier and was escaping.

"He may have dumped them in the Arkansas River or hauled them halfway to Kansas," said Lovelace.

Or the bodies could be lying a hundred miles east of Tulsa in Arkansas. Police homicide detectives Harold Haus and Ray Page pointed out that the cigarette package found in the car bore an Arkansas tax stamp.

More puzzling to the detectives was the reading on the car's speedometer—18,601 miles. A sticker on the door frame showed only 15,500 miles on the vehicle when it was lubricated at Paul's

Standard Service Station, in Hammond, on December 28, the day prior to the family's intended trek to New Mexico. The distance from Hammond to Tulsa was less than 600 miles. If the Hammond figures were correct, the Chevrolet had accumulated at least 2,400 additional miles that were unaccounted for.

Page called the station in Hammond. Paul Barnett, owner, verified servicing the sedan on Thursday.

"I didn't service it personally—one of my men did. He says he positively got the right figures on the sticker he pasted on the car. I can't understand it. I've known Carl all my life. He was a good and careful driver. Carl never would have driven an automobile like that—even if he could," Barnett told the detectives.

They had the speedometer inspected at the police garage, but the mechanism had not been tampered with.

The unexplained difference in mileage held fearful implications.

"The bodies of those people could be hundreds of miles from here," Haus concluded.

Deputy Smith and his posse continued to search the heavily wooded hills northwest of the city. "We'll keep scouring this neighborhood until we're satisfied," the deputy said.

Meanwhile, Detective Al DeMoss and County Investigator Ray Graves were clearing one point. Mosser's brother-in-law, Clarence Day, arriving with the relatives from Illinois, showed them a post card which his wife had received from Claremore, Oklahoma, postmarked at noon Saturday. It read:

Dear People—Having breakfast at the Will Rogers hotel in Claremore, on Route 66. We are seeing the USA in our Chevie ha. No trouble so far. X your fingers. Kids have done wonderful.
The Mossers

With Lieutenant Mosser, DeMoss and Graves drove to Claremore, twenty-seven miles northeast of Tulsa. Dorothy Belle Adair, a waitress at the hotel coffee shop, took one look at the missing man's twin and nodded.

"The little group was here on December 30. The man came in the coffee shop about 7 A.M., sat down and started reading a newspaper.

"Pretty soon, the woman and the three children came in. The

man helped the children off with their wraps, and helped them decide what to order.

"The children were such darlings—they kept running to look at the fish pond in the lobby while their orders were being prepared. While they were eating, the parents made them sit at the counter— but as soon as they were finished, they went to the lobby again to look at the fish.

"The man finished reading the paper and the woman wrote some postcards. When they left, I said 'Good-bye' to the little girl. Her mother said, 'Tell the lady bye,' and the child turned to me and said, 'Bye.'"

Miss Adair had not seen the Mossers again.

DeMoss and Graves admitted that the information was meager, but it shed light on when the family had disappeared.

Then developments in the case hit local and state newspapers, radio, and television. Pete Essley, Lloyd Edwards, the drugstore clerk, the taxi driver, and the barber related to police their experiences with the nervous youth seen near the automobile. Five witnesses gave similar descriptions. Essley remembered how he had kept one hand in his jacket pocket. All judged him to be twenty-five years old, five feet six or seven inches tall, weighing 150 pounds. The taxi driver recalled his thick lips and wavy brown hair. The barber described his muddy gray trousers and brown loafer shoes.

The suspect also had a "squint or droopy eye."

The police broadcast a statewide alert, urging all hunters, farmers, and motorists to report any suspicious person with these general characteristics.

In Oklahoma County, Sheriff Bob Turner checked the description against that of the droopy-eyed gunman who had robbed the Tahoka, Texas, mechanic of his car and money, and called Tulsa.

"There is a good chance that our cases are linked," the sheriff said.

Haus and Page rushed to Oklahoma City. They compared notes with Turner, and talked to state crime bureau agent Claud Seymour and farmer Kermit Mackey. Mackey repeated his story of how he had seen the gunman abandon his hijacking victim's machine and climb into an automobile carrying a man, woman, and three children—just at the time the Mossers, continuing west on U.S. 66 after eating breakfast at Claremore, would have been arriving in the Luther vicinity. Seymour described the Illinois car he had sighted later near Edmond.

Both men went with the detectives to Tulsa. Mackey looked at the blood-spattered Chevrolet and said it "resembled" the one he had seen near Luther.

"This is a 1949. The car I saw was a later model."

But Seymour was more positive. "It has the sun shade, red wind wings, and everything."

Significant, too, was the purchase slip of a .32 Colt automatic pistol found in the duffel bag left in Archer's vehicle. The bullets and cartridge cases recovered from the Mosser sedan were .32 caliber.

These factors spurred Oklahoma County officers in their effort to identify Archer's droop-eyed hijacker.

At the same time, Sheriff Turner asked county commissioners to instruct all highway department workers to make a thorough check of every country road—especially in the northeast section—for some sign of the missing family.

"Those men know every turn, every bridge, and every bend in those roads," the sheriff said. He also requested that road men in every county east of Oklahoma City do the same. "We think the man we are looking for got into the Mosser car," he explained. "If he did and if he killed those people as it now appears, the bodies could be anywhere between here and Tulsa."

Chief Norman Holt of the state highway patrol lent his support. He assigned all troopers between the two major cities to the hunt, and asked farmers living along U.S. 66, State 33, and all county roads extending off the two main highways to look under culverts, bridges, and in wooded areas.

As the search got under way, Deputy Burks filed a state armed robbery charge against "W. E. Cook, alias John Doe," based on the laundry marks of the T-shirts and the receipt for the purchase of the pistol.

"We're shooting in the dark in our assumption that the 'Cook' we are seeking is connected with the blood-stained car at Tulsa," Burks admitted. "But if he isn't the same man, it's one heck of a coincidence."

Immediately after the robbery charge was filed, D. A. Bryce, special agent in charge of the Federal Bureau of Investigation at Oklahoma City, filed a complaint before U.S. Commissioner Paul Showalter, charging "Cook" with "unlawful flight to avoid prosecution."

This action brought the facilities of the federal government into the investigation.

CHAPTER 7
BADMAN BILLY IDENTIFIED

Who was W. E. Cook? Was the name an alias? FBI teletype wires hummed to Washington as agents in Oklahoma City and Tulsa waited hopefully for a report from the bureau's voluminous criminal files.

Sheriff Turner had received no reply to his letter to the Kirksville, Missouri, studio seeking information on the framed portrait found in the duffel bag. Now that speed was necessary in identifying the man who had robbed Archer, he took the portrait to the newsroom of the *Daily Oklahoman*.

The *Oklahoman* sent the picture to St. Louis by Associated Press Wirephoto as a "special transmission" for the newspaper. It was not for publication. Then the St. Louis office of the FBI was notified that the picture was in the local wirephoto bureau, waiting for a federal agent to take it to Kirksville.

At Oklahoma City, Special Agent Bryce, in his typically close-mouthed manner, refused to comment on the photograph or its significance. However, within a matter of hours after the picture reached St. Louis, William Edward Cook Jr., twenty-three-year-old former Missouri convict of Joplin, was identified as the "Cook" wanted by the FBI. The three children in the portrait were his nephew and nieces. One of Cook's sisters had given him the photograph for Christmas, 1949, while he was still an inmate at the Jefferson City penitentiary.

Cook's criminal career was amply recorded on the Joplin police blotter and in the FBI files in Washington.

He had been dressed in at the State Training School for boys at Boonville on July 19, 1941, as a juvenile delinquent at the age of eleven. The sister at Kirksville and her husband had obtained his release in 1942, after he had served almost a year. His mother was dead. His seventy-year-old father, an old-age pensioner, lived in the suburbs of Joplin. He had "talked to Bill a lot about staying out of trouble." But Bill refused to go to school and was in hot water with the juvenile court most of the time. He hung around Joplin two years, went to the home of a sister in Texas, then came back again.

In September 1943, Carl Carrico, a Joplin taxi driver, had picked him up at a local motel.

According to Police Chief Frank Martin: "Cook flourished a pistol and ordered Carrico to drive to a lonely spot near the Kansas line. There he ordered Carrico to stop and take off his pants. He searched them and took $11. Then the fourteen-year-old gunman made Carrico drive him back to town. Cook then made him leave the cab again and ordered him to lie down. The cabbie refused. Cook whipped out a blackjack, administered a lick on each side of the cab driver's face, and left.

"The next day Carrico spotted him in front of a downtown theater. Cook tried to escape, but the cabbie overpowered him and shouted for the police. Cook had a gun stuck in his belt when arrested."

He had gone back to Boonville—this time for five years.

The reformatory, never exactly a finishing school for Little Lord Fauntleroys, was particularly a tough place in the early '40s. There were records of sexual immorality and later came charges of several attempted murders among inmates.

In this atmosphere of violence, "Cockeye Cook," also known as "Cookie," had made quite a name for himself.

Louis Bryant, a huge, friendly Negro patrolman on the Joplin police force, then a guard at Boonville, remembered him well:

"Once we caught him with a knife, sharp as a razor and made from a file six inches long. Another time he planned the burglary of

WANTED BY THE FBI

KIDNAPING
UNLAWFUL FLIGHT TO AVOID PROSECUTION (MURDER) (ROBBERY)

Photographs taken October 17, 1946   Photograph taken December, 1949

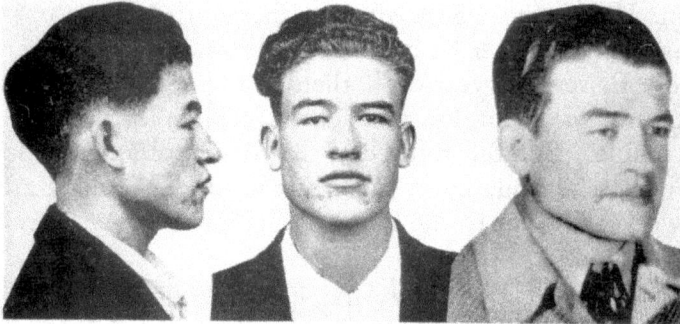

WILLIAM EDWARD COOK, JR.

with aliases: Bill Cook, Billy Cook, "Little Billy" Cook,
Bill Massengile, Bill Massengill, "Mr.'Reese"

DESCRIPTION

Age 23, born December 30, 1927, at Galena, Kansas; Height, 5'4½" to 5' 6"; Weight, 145 pounds; Build, medium; Hair, brown, wavy; Eyes, blue, one eye waters and eyelid droops; Complexion, fair to sallow, face may be pimpled; Race, white; Nationality, American; Scars and marks, numerous tattoos on arms including anchor with initials "R.S.S." and "W.E.C.", "Mary" and stars, "Steven" and flower petals, "Pat"; "HARD LUCK" tattooed on fingers; tattoo of moon on chest; 2" scar on upper lip; Remarks, Cook is known to have dyed his hair black and used crew style haircut in the past; he has never been known to wear a hat; usually wears dark glasses with shell rims.

FBI Number 3,753,404   Fingerprint Classification: 16 M I Uа 6 / S I R

CRIMINAL RECORD
COOK HAS PREVIOUSLY BEEN ARRESTED FOR HIGHWAY ROBBERY.

CAUTION
COOK IS ARMED, DESPERATE, AND EXTREMELY DANGEROUS. HE IS IN POSSESSION OF SEVERAL FIREARMS. HE IS WANTED FOR MULTIPLE MURDERS AND EXTREME CAUTION SHOULD BE EXERCISED IN APPREHENDING OR QUESTIONING HIM.

A complaint was filed January 7, 1951, before a U. S. Commissioner at Oklahoma City, Oklahoma, charging Cook with a violation of Title 18, U. S. Code, Section 1201, the Federal kidnaping statute.

Complaints were filed before U. S. Commissioners at Oklahoma City, Oklahoma on January 4, 1951 and at San Diego, California on January 7, 1951 charging Cook with violations of Title 18, U. S. Code, Section 1073 in that he fled from Oklahoma to avoid prosecution for the crime of robbery and fled from California to avoid prosecution for murder.

If you are in possession of any information regarding the whereabouts of this individual, please communicate with the undersigned, or with the nearest office of the Federal Bureau of Investigation, U. S. Department of Justice, the local address and telephone number of which are set forth on the reverse side of this notice.

JOHN EDGAR HOOVER, DIRECTOR
FEDERAL BUREAU OF INVESTIGATION
UNITED STATES DEPARTMENT OF JUSTICE
WASHINGTON, D. C.
TELEPHONE, NATIONAL 7117

Wanted Flyer No. 68 (Revised)
January 10, 1951

Wanted flyer posted by the FBI for Cook following his identification in connection with the kidnapping disappearance of the Carl Mosser family.

a dairy farm tenant's house, and the boys stole a gun there. He was the brains whenever there was trouble—always had criminal ideas on his mind."

Yet, when placed in solitary confinement for hitting an inmate from Kansas City over the head with a baseball bat, he had sobbed how his family did not seem to care for him and how he had no place to go.

Released from solitary, he had continued to be a major disciplinary problem.

"He threatened other boys and even officers," Bryant said. "He repeatedly planned escapes for others, preferring to stay behind and grow in stature as the planner who organized the job."

On March 23, 1946, Cook had participated in an escape himself. Naturally, he had organized it. Most of the boys had been caught immediately, but Cook remained at large until August 15, when he had the bad luck of running into Officer Bryant on a Joplin bus.

During the escape, he had tried to steal an automobile in Cooper County. He was now eighteen years old. He pleaded guilty to the attempted theft in the Cooper County Circuit Court, and received a term of five years in the Intermediate Reformatory at Algoa.

A month later, he had been caught trying to saw the bars for another escape. So he had been transferred to the state prison. He had been discharged June 16, 1950, after serving three-fourths of his sentence.

Since then, Cook had led a shadowy existence. "He came back to Joplin," said Chief Martin. "But one thing we appreciated is that he didn't stay around long."

At various times he had been reported in Kansas, Oklahoma, and Arkansas.

At Jefferson City, Warden Ralph N. Eidson remembered him as a "bad actor," but not bad enough to hold for his full five-year term.

"He was only caught in three violations—possession of benzedrine which had been smuggled into the prison, fighting with another inmate over a fountain pen, and finally, refusing to obey an order to leave the dining hall after the other prisoners left. Bill had to be taken out."

Whether Cook continued using benzedrine after his release or if it actually became a habit with him, the warden did not know.

"One thing certain, he's a well-marked man."

After his first trip to Boonville, Cook had employed a Joplin artist to tattoo an anchor on his arm, with the initials "R. S. S." and "W. E. C." Later, he had a moon put on his chest, and more tattoos on his arms, including flower petals and stars, and the names "Mary," "Steven," and "Pat."

"Tattooed across the fingers of his left hand are the letters H-A-R-D. He intended to have 'LUCK' tattooed on his right hand, but I think he abandoned the project," Eidson said.

The warden furnished the FBI's St. Louis office with Cook's latest photo, taken in 1943 when he was arrested at Joplin for armed assault and robbery. Within hours, several copies were in the hands of Oklahoma agents. Armed with photographs, the officers spread over the path of blood and violence.

In Oklahoma City, Seymour and Mackey admitted that neither had been close enough to the gunman to make an identification.

At Tulsa, Edwards, Murphy, the drugstore clerk, and barber said it "looked like" the man they had seen.

But Pete Essley shook his head. "This picture is seven years old. It would be pretty hard for anyone to be sure about a thing like that."

Tulsa police remained tight-lipped on the suspect being sought, and the FBI labeled the release of any such information "premature" until a positive identification could be made.

They rushed a copy of the photograph to Tahoka, Texas, to be shown Archer. But before they could get the Texas man's report, the Mosser tragedy hit newspapers throughout the Southwest. A call from Sheriff Hammett Vance of Wichita County sent Deputy Warren Smith and Ray Graves racing to Wichita Falls.

E. O. Cornwell repeated the story of how two men entered his store the night of December 30. "They began scuffling. I thought they were a couple of drunks. They broke out my window, so I got my gun and run them off. They were driving a dark blue Chevrolet with Illinois tags—like the one at Tulsa."

He looked at the picture of Carl Mosser with his family taken from the abandoned car. "It could have been him, but don't look much like him," Cornwell said. "This man has his hair parted wrong."

He studied the photograph of Cook. Again Cornwell hesitated. "The fellow in the leather jacket was more of a Mexican type. This isn't the same man."

The officers showed the pictures to Claude Skinner. But Skinner could see "no resemblance" to the men he had pursued halfway to Iowa Park.

Still hopeful, Smith and Graves had Lieutenant Mosser flown from Tulsa to Wichita Falls. In the office of Sheriff Vance, he was shown the hat bearing the label "The Famous Store, Decatur, Ill."

"The place where Carl bought all his clothing," Chris said. "My brother wore a size seven."

A few minutes later, Chris Mosser walked into the combination filling station-grocery store with the officers.

Cornwell looked at him, and exclaimed, "That's the man who screamed and grabbed the other fellow!"

"My twin brother," Lieutenant Mosser groaned miserably.

"I put out a pickup on the car as far as Amarillo," Sheriff Vance said, "but it never was sighted farther west than Iowa Park."

Rearing its ugly head now was the possibility that the family had been slaughtered in that area, before the car was returned to Tulsa.

Texas Rangers flew in from Dallas. Two carloads of FBI agents and state officers left Oklahoma for Wichita Falls. They met in Sheriff Vance's office to map plans for a new full-scale hunt for the bodies in the Wichita Falls vicinity.

And exactly at that moment, Mrs. Rufus Smith at Winthrop, Arkansas, was telling Deputy Sheriff Fred Harrelson of Ashdown how the family, accompanied by a droopy-eyed youth, who kept one hand in his jacket pocket, had stopped at her cafe on January 1 and bought cold drinks and sandwiches.

Smith and Graves left Wichita Falls at once by plane to Texarkana. From there, Texas Ranger Stewart Stanley drove them to Winthrop.

The way Graves told it later: "Mrs. Smith nearly fainted when we showed her Cook's picture. She identified him before she had time to put on her glasses. And Mrs. Sherman Tattle confirmed the identification."

Gradually, the accumulated mileage on the Mosser Chevrolet became clear. The family had traveled about 115 miles from Claremore to Luther before their nightmarish ride had begun. Wichita Falls was at least 200 miles beyond the point where Cook had entered the sedan. It was 300 miles from Wichita Falls to Winthrop and approximately 250 miles from Winthrop to Tulsa.

In all, the Chevrolet had traveled a known distance of 1,800 miles. The remaining 600 could have been driven between the family's appearance at Wichita Falls Saturday night and in Arkansas late Monday.

The vehicle apparently had traveled a complete circle, its trail obviously as bloody as the car itself.

Whatever had happened to the Mossers had occurred sometime during the night of January 1, or early January 2, before the car was discovered in Tulsa at 8:30 A.M.

Wichita Falls returned to normal as the score of visiting officers, news correspondents, and Texas Rangers shifted their activities to a wide range along the Oklahoma–Arkansas border.

Twenty planes fanned out from Tulsa and Winthrop, flying low over back roads, farm-to-market roads, and main highways between these points. The air search was augmented by twenty carloads of volunteers who streamed east and south across the interstate border. Twenty highway patrol units manned by fifty troopers and other officers were assigned to work in the field until the family was located. The natives of the hilly sections in both states offered their help, searching the area on horseback and afoot.

Huge posses headed by Sheriff Earl Kennon of Ashdown, Little River County, and Sheriff Cecil Dilhaunty of DeQueen, DeQueen County, gathered at Horatio, six miles north of the Winthrop community, and spread north and west through the wooded bottoms of Little River and Rolling Fork River on the theory that the Mossers had been slain and their bodies hidden before Cook got back into Oklahoma.

Sergeant Harold Porterfield of the Arkansas State Police and twelve troopers assigned to the hunt worked a thirty-mile strip from Mrs. Smith's cafe north to a point where U.S. Highway 70 entered Oklahoma near DeQueen.

"The Mossers had only forty-five minutes of daylight remaining when they left the cafe," Porterfield explained. "It is possible Cook allowed them to purchase drinks and sandwiches at the cafe—their last meal—then shot them to death shortly after dark."

They beat the strip thoroughly, checked bridges and culverts for bloodstains, and spread further north along U.S. 71, between DeQueen and Mena, without finding any trace of the family.

"We will extend the hunt to Fort Smith before we are through," Porterfield announced.

This was the "most probable" route taken by the gunman from Arkansas to Tulsa—U.S. 71 to Fort Smith, then on U.S. 64 into Oklahoma through Sallisaw and Muskogee, if he had remained on 64.

Another posse worked west along U.S. 70 between DeQueen and Broken Bow. Cook could have taken this route into Oklahoma, through Antlers, Atoka, Coalgate and on to Tulsa on U.S. 75 through Okmulgee.

Others covered Highways 63 and 270 west from Mena through the Ouachita National Forest into LeFlore County, a heavily wooded area.

In Tulsa, reports came from all sides—from gas station attendants, waitresses, and store clerks, who claimed to have seen the gunman. Every suspect with any characteristics of Cook's was picked up and questioned. None were jailed.

Several excited Tulsans called to determine what was required to own a gun for protection at home. More reported they were locking their doors securely hereafter.

Police assured nervous residents, however, that the fugitive apparently had not remained in that vicinity.

In other cities throughout eastern Oklahoma, local police radios constantly broadcast descriptions and other information on the former Missouri convict, considered a psychopathic killer by those close to the case.

Before the hunt was an hour old, state officers were hurrying to Okmulgee.

CHAPTER 8

SEARCH FOR THE BODIES FIZZLES

William Bennett, Okmulgee service station operator, told highway patrol troopers Kenneth Payne and Bill Cooper that a dark-colored Chevrolet carrying six persons fitting the general descriptions of Cook and the Mossers had stopped at his station the same night they were seen in Arkansas.

"This car pulled up just as I was closing—about 9 P.M.," Bennett said. "The driver got out, but he didn't leave the car. He stood by the window on the driver's side.

"There was another man, a woman, and three children in the Chevrolet," he added. "The other man was in the right front seat, the woman was in the rear seat on the right, and children were on the left.

"I didn't get a good look at them. But I'm positive the car was from Illinois because I asked the driver about coming down here from the cold weather.

"I put in seven gallons of gas, and he gave me a five. I thought he would come into the station to get his change, but he never left the side of the Chevrolet."

Bennett told the troopers that a photograph of Cook in the morning newspapers resembled the man who was at his station. "I can't positively say it was him because the picture is a little blurred.

"After I brought his change, he got back in the car and headed south toward Henryetta."

Two attendants at a service station on the east edge of Henryetta identified Cook as the man who had purchased gasoline from them more than an hour later.

Henry Porter and Jack Morgeson picked Cook's photograph from a group of three.

"He was driving a blue 1949 Chevrolet like the Mossers'," Morgeson told the troopers. "He was alone. His wavy hair bulged in front. He acted nervous. He also had a squint eye."

"The reason I remember him," Porter added, "he asked about buying some food."

They had directed him to the Earl Mumford grocery, a hundred yards up the highway from the station.

Mumford identified Cook as the man who had come to the store at 10:10 P.M.

"I'll never forget him," Mumford said. "He looked like a maniac. Kept staring like he was hypnotized. Nearly frightened my wife to death.

"I was working behind the counter and he walked right up in front of me. We almost bumped heads as I looked up at him, he got so close. He didn't say anything. Just stood there staring at me.

"I asked him what he wanted, and he replied, 'I don't want nothin'. I'm just warmin' myself.' But he never did stop staring at me.

"I never had a man look at me that way. His jaws kept going in and out like he was sucking his tongue or licking his lips. I thought he must be crazy or something. It was the first time in my seven years of running this store that I was scared.

"A lady customer came in, and I asked my wife to wait on her," Mumford continued. "I walked about forty feet in front of the counter to the door of our living quarters. I was going to get something to hit him with or at least get the difference. I could see the shape of a gun in his pocket and had a hunch he was going to rob us.

"He must have sensed what I was going after, for he left the store. The last I saw of him he was running toward the parked car at the service station."

Mumford could not recall his direction of travel. He thought he drove north, back toward Okmulgee.

"But I won't forget those eyes in a hundred years. I could pick them out of a thousand," the grocer concluded.

The fact that Cook had left Okmulgee with the Mossers but turned up alone in Henryetta indicated that his savage attack on the family had occurred somewhere on the fourteen-mile stretch of river bottom land between the two cities.

"It took him an hour and ten minutes to drive fourteen miles," Trooper Payne pointed out. "If our information is correct, he had at least forty-five minutes to dispose of the bodies."

The core of the hunt shifted to Okmulgee and Henryetta. Twelve additional highway patrol units commanded by Captain J. M. Thaxton of the southern Oklahoma district, two state crime bureau units, and five cars from the Federal Bureau of Investigation moved into the area. Osage Deputy Warren Smith and Ray Graves arrived from Arkansas to spearhead the search.

At the same time, a posse of more than eighty citizens headed south from Okmulgee, and another posse of fifty started north from Henryetta, covering U.S. 75 and side roads, tramping through ravines, and peering under culverts and bridges.

The hunt gained momentum when the posse from the south discovered a grimy envelope bearing the inscription "Ronnie 1950" alongside the highway four miles north of Henryetta.

Then, suddenly, the search shifted fifteen miles west to Okfuskee County.

Frank Been, who lived on Highway 62 four miles northeast of Okemah, reported that the family possibly had been slain near his home.

"My wife, Lena, and I were awakened about nine-thirty Monday night by two shots," Been, forty-five and part Indian, told Deputy Smith and Graves. "They were fired close to the house. There was a car out front, going west on the highway. I heard somebody scream. Like a kid, you know. There were three or more shots, then more screams.

"The shots were kind of little, not like a big gun. More like a .32."

The car had gone west about a mile and turned around near the home of a neighboring farmer, Bill Wheeler. Wheeler told the officers the lights from the car had awakened him, but he could not identify its make or model.

"It came back past my house," Been said. "I couldn't see the car very well, but it sounded like a good one."

Been had thought it was some boys celebrating New Year's. "I didn't connect the shots with this missing family till I heard you were looking for them down here."

The time element jibed with Cook's other appearances in the area. If he had killed the Mossers at 9:30 P.M., he still had forty minutes to dispose of them and drive the fifteen miles from Been's farm to Mumford's store at Henryetta.

Sparked by the certainty of the time and place of the family's fate, more than a hundred grim-faced hunters gathered near Been's farm. A systematic search—both from the air and on the ground—fanned out in all directions.

Smith and Graves urged all farmers in the vicinity of Okemah to check their land for the bodies.

After an exasperating seven hours, they saw three of their most important leads fizzle.

The envelope found beside the highway proved to have no connection to the case. It had been addressed to a boy who formerly lived in Henryetta.

The significance of the statement of Frank Been dwindled when another farmer living near Been's home told state troopers that a horse had been shot on his farm five times with a .22 rifle on New Year's night.

Hopes further dimmed when William Bennett, taken to Tulsa and shown the Mosser sedan, said it was not the car he had serviced at Okmulgee.

Unshaken, however, were the reports of the two service station attendants and the grocer and his wife at Henryetta.

The highway patrol made a final effort. Troopers Hamilton and Wiley Burris spent the rest of the day flying low over U.S. 62 east to Henryetta; U.S. 75 north through Okmulgee to Sapulpa, Sand Springs and Tulsa; both banks of the Arkansas River to Muskogee; U.S. 64 from Muskogee back to Tulsa; then U.S. 66 to Bristow, and State Highway 21 from Bristow south through Castle to Okemah.

They searched particularly for any concentration of crows or buzzards.

The original hunt started in Arkansas and southeastern Oklahoma continued.

Oklahoma's state safety commissioner, Coble Gambill, urged

troopers to check all gas stations to learn if a man fitting Cook's description had refilled the tank of the Mosser vehicle.

"We know he bought gasoline close to Tulsa as the tank on the car was full. It is important to know where he bought it, and if the family was still with him."

At the same time, he made the following appeal to citizens:

"In case you should be the one to find the bodies of the Mossers, report your discovery promptly.

"Then, go back to the scene, but DON'T tamper with anything; DON'T permit anyone to tramp around; DON'T let anyone go close enough to mess up footprints or tire tracks or other clues.

"We must keep the killer of these people from going free if he can be captured. Even the most insignificant thing may become vital evidence."

This brought a new rash of leads.

Detectives Cecil Ray and Jim Gott raced to a spot beyond the Verdigris River on U.S. 66 near Claremore after a nervous caller had seen a butchered baby girl wrapped in paper and lying in a ditch, bloody and dissected.

The Tulsa detectives found the paper, but the contents proved to be the neckbone of a hog.

Another uneasy Tulsan called police to tell them that Cook had just been found dead in a car in a heavily wooded section of Mohawk Park. It turned out that a young soldier from Iowa had committed suicide by breathing carbon monoxide fumes from his exhaust.

Others, anxious to provide a clue, brought in old shoes, blankets, jugs, and other items found along various highways. Few actually fit into the pattern.

An exception was noted, however. Traffic Officer L. E. Kidwell headed a party that discovered a bloody shirt, a blood-stained pillow, and a thermos bottle, like the one used by the Mossers, on the Old Hill Road a mile west of Sand Springs. The items apparently were possessions of the family.

These tied in with another late development in the case. A laboratory analysis of a muddy footprint found near the abandoned car in the Osage Hills showed the soil chemically resembled that of the Sand Springs-Sapulpa area.

Obviously Cook had tried to bypass Tulsa through Sapulpa and Sand Springs then wound up stuck on the Osage County road.

Four search parties fanned out from Tulsa, sweeping wide sections beyond the city into Creek County and back through the Osage Hills.

Another party began combing the area to Keystone along the Arkansas River, east and west of the Sapulpa-Sand Springs cut-off. County Commissioner Claude Bailey and his thirty-five highway employees inched southeast toward Leonard and Broken Arrow. Fifteen boat enthusiasts left the river bridge at Sand Springs to float to Jenks in a further attempt to locate bodies. A few hours later, the hunt was being concentrated along the interstate border near Fort Smith.

Detectives Haus and Page had gone from Tulsa to Winthrop to recheck the articles found in the Mosser car. "We didn't have to show Mrs. Smith what was in the Chevrolet," Haus said later, "she knew. She not only identified the soft drink bottles, the thermos jug and fruit jar, she furnished us an itemized list of what Mosser purchased."

The wrappers and sticks from ice cream bars had not come from the cafe. The ice cream bars were manufactured by a Fort Smith firm. A check with the firm showed their product was not distributed over fifty miles from the city in any direction.

CHAPTER 9

"LIVE BY THE GUN, AND ROAM"

While hundreds searched for the Mossers in Arkansas and Oklahoma, a team of FBI agents moved into Joplin. Here Cook had been reared. Here they hoped to find the bit of information that would result in his apprehension.

Easy dough. You've got to take it the hard way. I'm going to live by the gun, and roam.

This was Bill Cook's credo.

"Bill thought life had given him a kick in the seat of the pants," said Joplin's chief of detectives, Carl Nutt. "He's been trying to kick it back ever since."

Trouble had begun for the runty little criminal at birth. He came into the world on December 3, 1928, with a large, ugly growth covering his right eye. It did not impair his eyesight, but he had to lift the lid with his fingers in order to see.

He was a skinny baby. His first teeth decayed as fast as they popped out. He had a lot of stomach trouble and difficulty in keeping food down. There was very little food around the house anyway. Mostly, the Cook brood whiled away the time in one-room hovels that cluttered the mining area on the west edge of the city, waiting for red-letter days when friends and relatives would bring in a few vegetables or biscuits. They called the biscuits cake.

There were eight children—four girls older than Bill, two younger sisters and a younger brother. Bill was the quiet, bashful one. He talked little, kept his face down, blushed easily and never was noted for cursing.

He loved his younger sisters and brother. His mother always could trust him to look after them, and when they got in trouble, Bill would say, "I don't want you to spank them, I want you to spank me first."

He hadn't changed much, even after coming back from prison.

"He's sullen and speaks in a low monotone—when he talks," Nutt said. "We never did consider him dangerous. Just a hard one to figure."

All the Cook children were alive, married, and working—scattered over several states. The sister at Kirksville had married a Salvation Army captain once stationed in Joplin. She had kept in touch with Bill during his stays in prison and done more than the others trying to help him after their mother died and the family broke up completely.

Bill's mother died when he was five. Her name was Laura Steven, and she had four children by a previous marriage when Will Cook showed up as a sharecropper on her father's cotton farm near Webber Falls, Oklahoma, during World War I.

Later, the family moved to Joplin, where Will went to work in the Eagle-Picher mines carting wheelbarrows piled high with slag. Never a big man, but strong as an ox, he could haul the biggest load of anyone. But he only worked occasionally, and never earned enough to provide for his family.

Will left his wife and children in 1933. Laura was recovering from a stroke, when one day she was cutting kindling wood. A stick leaped high, striking her between the eyes. Though weak from the blow, she walked calmly into the house and told Bill and the other children that she was lying down for a nap.

Hours later, when the children became hungry, Bill ran into a neighbor's house, crying, "Mommie went to sleep and we can't wake her up."

She was dead.

Shortly afterward, the local truant officer learned that a gang of ragged kids was living in a cave of the abandoned White Shirt lead mine located in uninhabited timberland a half-mile off the highway outside Joplin. He and Mrs. Vernie Goff Bryson, chief probation officer for Jasper County from 1933 to 1945, went to the mine and found Bill and his sisters and brother.

"I've handled hundreds of court children in my time," Mrs. Bryson told the agents, "but I'll never forget the sight I saw in that cave seventeen years ago.

"The children were living by themselves in this cave. It used to be a 'doghouse' where the miners changed clothes. They had a set of rusty bedsprings with a mattress, a kerosene lamp and an old ax they were going to use to defend themselves. Imagine that! They had some kind of stove and on it was an uncovered can of pancake batter. When one of them got hungry, one of the older girls would make a pancake. They drank water standing in an old mine shaft outside.

"The court policy on children was, 'Get rid of 'em, put them in homes so we wouldn't have to pay the fifteen-dollars-a-month support on each child. Those were depression days and fifteen dollars covered everything—food, shelter, clothing. When the father came for the children, we let him have them."

But Will Cook soon left his children again—this time in an abandoned blacksmith shop between Chitwood and Smelter Hill.

"I was called at night, when we were having one of those ice storms like we get up here," Mrs. Bryson remembered, "and I found them in this place with the storm blowing right through the boards. Those children were blue. They would have frozen to death before morning. And you wonder why Bill grew up and got in trouble!"

This time the court persuaded Will Cook to release the children from his care "now and forever." The children were separated. All of them found permanent foster homes—except Bill.

He was shuttled from family to family. Nobody wanted him. They were afraid his deformed eye harbored some kind of disease. Welfare officers arranged for an operation.

Ellsworth Moody, a kindly bachelor who cared for wards of the Jasper County court without ever sending a bill, removed the growth. The operation was not completely successful. The eyelid drooped.

Bill was placed in a boarding home. The owners, who tried to give him love and affection, finally adopted him.

He was eleven now. He attended school fairly regularly and

got a bicycle for Christmas. The bicycle was taken when the credit installments were not paid.

The pint-sized youngster, his clothes under one arm and a purposeful glint in his eye, called on the county judge.

"I won't live at that place any more," he said. "They took my bike."

The judge sent him home. Bill got another bicycle. But he was dissatisfied and restless. He sold the bicycle for two dollars, and ran away. Caught and brought back to the court, he claimed he had been mistreated.

The court sent him to live with an older married sister. Within ten days, he was before the judge again. His sister accompanied him. She said he was unruly, went into tantrums, and was unmanageable.

"He did not have a nickel's worth of clothes and what he had on was dirty enough to stand alone," the court record entry read. And it added: *"Bill is not a bad boy."*

He was placed in another home. He got another bicycle and went back to school—for a while.

"He was sly and cunning," recalled Miss Ethel Masters, principal and teacher at the Jefferson school where Bill was her sixth-grade pupil. "He stole little things and blamed other boys. He didn't care about the trouble he caused others as long as he got what he wanted. He had more than average intelligence, but took little interest in his lessons. His grades were about average."

She produced a photograph of Jefferson's sixth-grade class taken in 1940. Bill Cook, his face wearing a disarming grin, stared back from the upper left corner of the picture.

"He had what you call a 'poker face,'" said E. O. Humphrey, the truant officer at the time. "He was a lone wolf with a vicious streak—a tough little kid who kept me busy. When he passed to the seventh grade, he announced that he was 'through with school.'"

On July 15, 1941, his latest foster mother returned Bill to the probation office. He was booked as "incorrigible."

Judge Wilbur Owen gave the boy a choice—straighten up and attend school regularly or be committed to the reformatory.

"You can stay in a home, and we'll let you choose the home," the judge said.

"I'll not stay any place you put me," Bill declared.

Judge Owen sentenced him to one year at Boonville.

The FBI agents knew the rest of the story. They needed to pick up his trail after his release from Jefferson City.

Cook's sister and brother-in-law from Kirksville had met him at the prison gates. "He promised to stay out of trouble," his sister said. "He told us that he had 'enough of those places' and seemed genuinely glad to be free."

He bought candy and presents for his nieces and nephew. His wavy hair was his pride and joy. He kept it neatly trimmed, used a lot of perfumed oil on it, and stopped frequently in front of a mirror to comb it and put the curls in place. He tried to find a job, but no one wanted him because of his record. He tried to join the Army and Navy. Again his record interfered. He stayed in Kirksville two weeks, then drifted to Joplin.

Among the abandoned mines, in the middle of a desolate wind-swept field hugging the city limits, Bill had made his last stop—the shack of old Will Cook, his father.

It was a windowless one-room shack, measuring perhaps eight by twelve feet. There were scores of others like it in Chitwood and adjoining Smelter Hill, where families used outside privies and shivered as the wind whipped through the wide cracks below the doors and ruffled the rags that littered floors.

Will's shack, for which he had paid $150 including the lot, stood in the apex of a V formed by two sets of railroad tracks meeting just beyond. One track ran into Joplin, the other to the Eagle-Picher refinery and Smelter Hill. Once lead and zinc had been mined in the city limits. Now only tired old Bull Frog Cave was being worked.

Will Cook sat inside his shack, chewing tobacco, worrying about his old-age pension check and the bees he was trying to raise, and reading a copy of a Western magazine by the light of a single yellow bulb.

The walls were insulated with cardboard torn from abandoned grocery cartons. Balls of dusty blankets smothered a creaky bed in one corner. Dirt-caked dishes and jars covered a rickety table. Almost every inch of floor space groaned under the load of old boxes, suitcases, and piles of unwashed clothing. There hardly was room for two federal agents inside the door. Chief Nutt and Detective Walter Gamble, who accompanied them, waited outside.

Asked about his son, the old man remembered how Bill had come home "last summer" more embittered than ever.

"There was somethin' funny about the boy. Acted like he was stir-happy. He said he wasn't ever gonna be arrested no more. The first man even looks like he's gonna arrest him he was gonna shoot him down. I was afraid of him."

Will Cook laid down his magazine and stared at the agents without moving from his chair. He wore wrinkled khaki trousers, a black leather jacket, a green cowboy shirt, and a grease-stained cowboy hat. His feet peeked out of the sides of his shoes. His haggard face was set in hard, deep lines.

"I don't know where the boy is now," Will continued. "If I did I'd tell you, before he gets hisself killed."

In fact, he had had little or no contact with any of his children since welfare authorities found the abandoned brood, ill-clothed and near starvation in the mine area cave.

"Bill ain't ever comin' back home nohow," Will said. "He wanted me to throw in with him, and I turned him down."

He said his son had proposed a partnership in crime.

"'They owe us a living and I'm goin' to get it,' he sez to me. 'I'll get a gun, knock off a few places around here, you can say I was home in bed.' But," the old man added proudly, "I sez I won't alibi for nobody. So he sez he's goin' to Wichita, Kansas. Maybe Colorado."

The agents explored the possibility that Will Cook's son had fled back to Missouri after abandoning the Mosser car near Tulsa, and was hiding in the Joplin area.

Will Cook "doubted that," but agreed to cooperate in any way he could.

At the request of Detectives Nutt and Gamble, the old man went on the radio. "Now, Bill," he drawled into the microphone, "this is your dad in Joplin. I wish you'd give yourself up. If you give yourself up and come home here, I'll guarantee you won't get shot. If you don't come in, you're gonna get killed. So, Bill, please come home."

Chief Nutt joined in the broadcast, assuring the youth he would personally take him into custody, and that he would not be harmed if he surrendered promptly.

But the old man's plea and the detective's promise were in vain.

The search for Cook continued in Missouri. The FBI pin-pointed the locations of known friends and relatives in other states, and had their homes watched. They blanketed the country with "wanted" circulars showing front and profile views of Cook, and the same photographs appeared on the front pages of metropolitan newspapers.

On a Thursday night, a service station operator at Pittsburg, Kansas, twenty-five miles from Joplin, reported that he sold gasoline to a man resembling Cook who was driving a green 1947 Chevrolet sedan bearing Missouri plates.

Two hours later, the town of Cherryvale, fifty miles northwest, was in an uproar after a woman reported a man answering Cook's description approached her car in what she thought was an attempt to kidnap her.

She told Police Chief Albert Clark that she grabbed her car keys and fled into her mother's home before the man could stop her. Chief Clark said, "The whole town is aroused, and the police station is filled with people who want guns."

Still later that night, a statewide alarm was sounded for a gunman who tried to steal an automobile from a garage at McCook, Nebraska, then wounded Deputy Sheriff Fran Dolan during a wild, ninety-five-mile-an-hour chase.

Sheriff Emmett Trosper said the fugitive "might be Cook," since the sedan in which the gunman escaped was coated with gray mud, indicating it recently had been driven from Missouri.

By Friday morning a man believed to be the desperado was fleeing across South Dakota after spending the night at a Worthington, Minnesota, hotel, seventy miles east of Sioux Falls.

Heavily armed state highway patrolmen set up roadblocks on every route between Sioux Falls and Sioux City, Iowa, and scores of police joined the manhunt at other points

Another report, received late in the day, placed Cook at Sundown, Texas, forty-five miles west of Lubbock, where he had entered the car of his first victim, Archer. A masked man had forced his way into a home, grabbed food from a kitchen table, and fled.

And a hitchhiker told El Paso police he had ridden at night across West Texas with a short, stocky man about Cook's age, who had kept a pistol on the seat between them.

The FBI built files, ran down the leads, and indexed every

movement of the wanted man. Agents frankly were at a loss to explain how Cook—if it was he—got so many places in thirty hours.
The reports were reminiscent of the days when Pretty Boy Floyd
was "robbing banks two hundred miles apart" at the same hour.

But one report interested them. Across the Mexican border, a
frightened nightclub dancer went to the Juarez police with her
story of the droopy-eyed gunman's promise to return; she asked for
protection. She remembered where Cook told her he had spent
Christmas day.

A special alert spread to California.

CHAPTER 10
THE HUNT IN CALIFORNIA

At Blythe, a small town in the southern California desert near the Arizona border, Deputy Sheriff Homer Waldrip saw an FBI flyer and recognized the youth who had washed dishes in a local cafe two weeks previously.

Waldrip was a twenty-nine-year-old, heavy-set, dark-haired man with a thin mustache and high forehead, the father of two small daughters. He had been a deputy for Riverside County only a short time, was a former Blythe policeman, and an experienced officer.

There was no question about the dishwasher's identity. Waldrip's wife worked at the same cafe. The deputy ate there and had seen Cook when he first appeared in Blythe on December 3.

Cook had labored briefly at $45 a week. On Christmas day he left Blythe with a middle-aged waitress and her husband on a trip to Juarez, Mexico.

"Bill had an idea he could 'buy' a Mexican girl south of the border and import her into this country," the waitress had told fellow employees. "He found a girl, but she couldn't come with us because she had no passport. We left Bill in El Paso."

Waldrip remembered that Cook had lived in a nearby motel with a man named Paul Reese. He thought Reese might supply a lead to his friend's whereabouts. After taking his wife to work, the deputy drove to the motel. It was shortly after 9:00, Saturday morning, January 6.

Waldrip knocked at Reese's door and a voice said, "Come in."

He opened the door. As he stepped inside, someone rammed a gun into his ribs.

"Stick 'em up, deputy!"

Waldrip raised his hands and looked around into the face of droopy-eyed Bill Cook!

"What's the idea!" he demanded, managing to conceal his surprise. "Is this a joke of some kind?"

Cook, facing him with a pistol, grinned a bit foolishly. "You remember me, don't you?" he asked.

"No. I don't remember you," Waldrip hedged. "I'm looking for Paul."

Cook studied him a moment, cocked his head to one side, then said, "You remember me all right, and I know why you're here."

He removed Waldrip's .38 service revolver from its holster and shoved it down in his belt under his jacket. Then he forced the deputy back to his patrol car and climbed in beside him.

"Get going!" he said, in a low, savage voice. "Drive where I tell you. Try any funny business, and I'll blast hell of you!"

Waldrip stepped on the starter and backed the car out of the driveway. "Where do you want me to go?" he asked.

"Drive west—on Highway 60."

Waldrip drove along the highway through the residential section. As they approached the cafe where his wife was working, Cook told him to speed up. "You wouldn't want anyone to see us," he said. His droopy eyelid lifted a trifle as he continued to grin.

Waldrip's face paled a little, and he gripped the steering wheel tightly. With an automatic trained on his ribs, it was no time to argue. He wondered what Cook's intentions were.

Four miles west of Blythe, they passed an intersection known as Ripley Corner. "Turn around," Cook ordered. "Go back to the corner and take the road to the desert."

Waldrip drove back to the corner and turned south on a utility road. Six miles further, they passed through Ripley. From there the road jogged southwest to Palo Verde, another desert stop between Yule Mountains and the Colorado River.

"Call the sheriff on your radio," Cook said. "I want to talk to him."

Waldrip tried to call the dispatcher at Riverside. He couldn't get through because of interference.

Cook didn't like that. Waldrip figured he wanted to taunt the sheriff.

As they reached the outskirts of Palo Verde, Waldrip pointed to the fuel guage.

"I guess we won't get much further," he announced. "We are about out of gas."

Suspicious, Cook leaned slightly forward and looked. The hand was riding on empty.

"We'll get some here," he said.

Waldrip was thinking fast. At a service station, maybe he would get a chance to tell the attendant of his plight. Cook was thinking along the same lines.

"Like I told you back there," he warned, "don't try any funny stuff. If you try to wise up the fellow at the filling station, I'll kill you and him both. Understand? Now drive into that station over there."

"Sure," said Waldrip dryly, "I understand."

He swung the cruiser into the station Cook pointed out.

"Fill it up," Cook told the attendant.

Waldrip tried to catch the man's eye, but he already had gone to the rear of the car to put gasoline into the tank.

"I don't have enough money," he explained to Cook.

Cook reached in his own pocket, handed the deputy a ten dollar bill and waited for the attendant to return with the change.

Waldrip winked at the attendant in a desperate effort to let him know something was wrong. The man didn't savvy. He thanked the deputy for his business and turned back to his pumps.

As the ride continued, Waldrip's hopes died. The next town was Ogilby, forty-five miles southwest through the Chocolate Mountains and deserts of Imperial County and ten miles north of the Baja California border. It was a lonely section of country, and the roads over which he was compelled to drive were traveled very little, many of them scarcely more than trails.

A few miles out of Palo Verde, one trail led east to the Colorado River, then south along the Arizona border to intersect

U.S. Highway 80, which ran east and west between Yuma and El Centro, parallel with the Mexican border. Several miles south, another led west to Glamis, in the sand hills.

Cook was studying a road map he had found in the glove compartment. "Take me to Yuma," he decided, "and make it fast!"

Waldrip drove in silence. All the time, Cook kept talking.

"Want to know why I'm doing this? Well, I'll tell you. I started home to Missouri. I caught a ride in Texas and a man jumped me. I thought he was trying to take my money, so I put my gun on him, and he got away.

"I went on from there till his car burned up, then picked up the Mosser family, but I had to kill them."

Cook paused to read the effect of his announcement. Waldrip said nothing. The desert rolled past under the speeding cruiser.

"Don't tell me you haven't heard about that, deputy? I killed the whole family and buried the bodies in the snow in Oklahoma where nobody can find them. I killed them because I saw Mosser wink at his wife sitting in the back seat with three kids."

Cook chuckled. It was an ugly sound. And Waldrip wondered if he'd seen him wink at the service station attendant in Verde.

"I was tired and sleepy," Cook continued. "Mosser slammed on the brakes and pitched his wife into the front seat against me.

"I started firing. The first shot hit Mosser, the second hit his wife. One shot went wild and hit a kid. That started them crying, so I killed them all.

"I killed two more on my way to California," he claimed. But he didn't identify the victims. "You'll be number eight," he said. His droopy eyelid twitched.

"No need to kill me," Waldrip said. "Just take my car."

Cook didn't answer.

As they approached Highway 80, Cook changed his mind. He ordered Waldrip to turn around and take another trail back into the desert.

Waldrip drove north and then west, until they reached the main road to Ogilby. Cook told him to turn south again.

"Flag the first car we meet. Use your red light," he said.

They didn't meet another car.

At a crossroads known as Desert Well, Cook told him to turn off into the desert again.

Two miles further, it came—the order Waldrip had been dreading. "This place is okay. Stop the car!"

Cook got out on the right side and ordered the deputy to follow him.

"Now," he said, "put your hands on top of the car with your feet way out."

Waldrip complied. There was nothing else to do. Cook stood behind him. The pistol gouged his back.

He felt the killer remove his wallet. Waldrip knew it contained $130. He had cashed his county check that morning.

Cook found the money. He threw the wallet on the ground and started cursing. "Goddamn you, deputy, you lied!"

Waldrip had no doubts that Cook would kill him now. He could almost feel the bullet ripping through his body.

Then Cook asked if he had a rope or anything he could use to tie him.

Waldrip relaxed, temporarily. "There's a blanket in the trunk," he offered.

"Get it."

Waldrip got the blanket. Cook tore it into strips. Keeping his pistol trained on the deputy's heart, he ordered him to lie face down in the sand.

"Why don't you give me a break?" Waldrip pleaded.

"What kind of break?" Cook snarled.

"You have my car and money. Give me a break."

"Why should I? Nobody ever gave me a break," Cook replied.

He ordered Waldrip to cross his hands behind him. Holding the pistol in one hand, he bound the deputy's wrists with the other.

"I'm not going to tie your feet. It won't be necessary," he said. *"I didn't tie the feet of the others."*

Cook poised the gun. Waldrip felt it touch the back of his head. He buried his face in the sand to hide the tears that suddenly welled in his eyes. What a hell of a way to die, without even a chance to defend himself. He thought of his wife, Cecilia, and their two little girls.

He never knew why Cook didn't pull the trigger. Instead, the killer rose and walked back to the car. Waldrip heard him slam both doors. The starter ground over, and then for several moments there was a roar as he sat there racing the motor.

He wondered if Cook was waiting to see if he was going to lift his head or turn over. Those seconds were long until he heard the car drive away. When he finally raised his head, the killer had vanished in the wastelands.

It took Waldrip only a few minutes to free himself of the blanket strips. He hurried back to the highway. Tracks in the sand showed Cook had turned toward Ogilby. Waldrip walked north toward Palo Verde. Six miles and thirty minutes later, he was picked up by two border patrolmen from Yuma.

The three officers swung back, thinking to catch Cook on the desert road. They drove for some time. Seven miles north of Ogilby they saw Waldrip's cruiser parked alongside the highway.

They spread out in a wide circle and approached the car with guns drawn. There was no one about. The ignition was on and the red light was still burning.

They could see tracks in the road where another automobile coming from the south had turned around. Obviously Cook had used the red light to stop his latest victim.

Waldrip started his cruiser and the three men headed for Ogilby to flash an alarm.

A mile further, they came upon the body of a man sprawled in the sand. He had been shot through the back and right side. He was dead.

CHAPTER 11
FLIGHT TO MEXICO

The dead man was Robert H. Dewey, 32, an employee of a Seattle, Washington, oil company.

"I can't believe it!" exclaimed his wife at Seattle when informed that her husband had been slain. He had served two years overseas during World War II, had been wounded in France shortly after D-day, was a Purple Heart veteran, and a captain in the Army Reserve. "He probably stopped to help this man—Cook. He'd always do that if he thought someone was in trouble on the highway.

"And death is what he got."

Mrs. Louise Dewey, a former newspaperwoman, had just returned from visiting her parents in Illinois. "Bob left home last Wednesday and expected to return next week," she explained.

He had gone down to Spring Valley, California, to visit his father and stepmother, who had recently moved there from Elmhurst, and to revisit the desert where he had trained with armored units of the Seventh Infantry Division.

"He enjoyed the terrain and climate very much and always wanted to go back. But now I wish he had never gone on this miserable adventure."

At nearby Spring Valley, his grief-stricken father told police his son had left early that morning for a hunting trip in the Chocolate

Mountains. He had been driving a blue 1947 Buick torpedo sedan loaded with a camp stove, blankets, a .54-caliber Winchester and .22 bolt-action rifle, and enough food supplies for a week. The car bore a 1950 Washington license plate number A-122471.

At least four roads lay open to Cook west of Yuma. The FBI, California highway patrol, Arizona State Police, and local officers set up blockades on all of them. The border patrol slapped a close guard on all three highway exits to Mexico.

The first broadcasts cut off escape further west through California. Federal, state, and local officers all believed Cook's most logical path of flight was north and east from the Ogilby vicinity.

At El Centro, Sheriff Robert W. Ware, of Imperial County, threw three men into the field and alerted a hundred reservists to stand by.

In Riverside County, the sheriff's aero squadron launched an area-wide search that would extend into the rugged Chocolate, Palo Verde and Chuckawalla mountain ranges to the northwest.

At Phoenix, Arizona, Sheriff Cal Boies ordered out his air posse of seventeen planes to cover the vast, sparsely settled triangle of mountain ranges and desert between Phoenix, Blythe, and Yuma.

It was now past noon. Cook had at least a half-hour's head start. In Dewey's Buick he could have driven east through Yuma or doubled back through Blythe and crossed the Colorado at Ehrenberg before the initial roadblocks were established.

Bloodhounds from the Arizona state prison at Florence were flown to the area to be put on Cook's trail in the event he abandoned the car and attempted to hide in the deserts—should he be that foolish.

The desert stretches two hundred miles west of Phoenix. Anyone venturing into it on foot must surely perish, Sheriff Boies believed.

He was sure they had the fugitive in a giant trap. They must close its steely fingers slowly and carefully, lest the sawed-off Missouri desperado slip through.

News of the kidnapping of Waldrip and the murder of Dewey had spread throughout the border country. Radio stations in southern California broadcast frequent descriptions of the much-sought killer, and his picture was televised at intervals.

The next twelve hours were a hectic period. Well-meaning citizens reported a man resembling Cook in half a dozen hideouts. Every squad was kept busy checking tips, and they kept a wire open to Sheriff Ware's office at El Centro, the focal point of all information and activity.

By midnight Saturday, with no word of the fugitive, it began to look as though their fine theories had been haywire. Sheriff Ware had placed roadblocks the length and breadth of the Imperial Valley, from the Mexican border to the Salton Sea, and stopped all cars except those driven by local people known to the officials.

In Yuma and Maricopa counties, in Arizona, authorities had made every effort to locate Cook. A killer-at-large was nothing new to them. In 1949, Billy Ray Gilbert, another maddog slayer who killed three persons, was mowed down by Phoenix policemen with machine guns. Five armed robbers had been captured in the area within the past ten days. Residents, aware their section appeared to be a mecca for fleeing murderers and hijackers, cooperated 100 percent with the authorities. They had turned the southwestern corner of the state inside out, and they were positive Cook was not in their jurisdiction.

William A. Murphy, FBI chief in Arizona, doubted that Cook had crossed the Colorado River. Some feared he had escaped over the international border, but Murphy pointed out that he did not speak Spanish and would have had difficulty getting past border patrols.

He suggested that perhaps the fugitive had headed for the mountains of Imperial and Riverside counties. "He has enough food and camping paraphernalia to provide a perfect setup for a prolonged mountain hideout if he can reach either of those ranges. He must have gone that way."

But Sheriff Ware stuck to the original theory that he had not left the wastelands between Ogilby and Blythe. "The roadblocks were erected in plenty of time to keep him inside our net. He might be camped out in some hidden desert wash but he can't stay there long without water. We are expecting to establish contact with him at any moment."

In any event, both officials were confident Cook had enough ammunition to offer a lengthy battle for any pursuers who came upon him, and had little doubt he would kill again before he would submit to arrest.

His arsenal now consisted of four guns—Dewey's Winchester and bolt-action rifles, his own .32 automatic and Waldrip's .38 revolver.

Cook's confession to Waldrip that he had slain Carl Mosser, his wife, and three children and "buried them in the snow" had Oklahoma officers baffled. It had snowed only as far east as Pawnee on Tuesday, the day the family's bloodstained Chevrolet was first seen near Tulsa.

Other towns receiving snow that day, according to the weather bureau, were Kingfisher, Enid, Boise City, and Clinton, in the western part of the state.

There were snow flurries in the mountains of southeastern Oklahoma near the Arkansas line on New Year's Eve, but forest rangers said only rain had fallen there on Monday.

"By the time the family left Winthrop, there wasn't a sign of a snowflake in the area," Otis Hall, district forester at Broken Bow, reported.

The highway patrol, discouraged after four days of fruitless search, decided to start all over again—at Luther, where Cook had flagged down the Mosser car.

"The family and Cook have been seen in so many places," said Commissioner Gambill, "we are apt to find those bodies anywhere now. So we're going to retrace the whole route."

There was a growing feeling among officers, however, that the family would not be found until their killer revealed where he had hidden them.

Sunday morning, January 7, California officers got their first important lead on Cook in Imperial County. A late model blue Buick sedan was checked through the Yuma agricultural inspection station at 2:35 A.M. Too late, officials noticed that its license plate was missing.

A deputy sheriff sighted the sedan speeding west on U.S. 80. He fired two shots as the vehicle approached his blockade and failed to halt.

Two highway patrol troopers saw the car turn off on Highway 98 and gave pursuit. Driving without lights, at speeds up to one hundred miles an hour, it outran them on the thirty-six-mile stretch to Calexico and disappeared in the desert south of Mexicali.

Despite all efforts, Cook had succeeded in crossing the international border.

CHAPTER 12
KIDNAPPING OF DAMRON AND BURKE

Baja California is a region of few roads and poor communications, truly "a land of tomorrow." It is a country of various moods and atmospheres. Like the country, its people also live greatly contrasting lives.

Mexicali, the capital of the North District of the province, with 75,000 population, sprawls just across the border, nineteen miles south of El Centro. It sleeps in the desert sun like a giant toad, but it is the most progressive city in the peninsula.

A visit to Mexicali is a must for everyone who comes to Imperial Valley for a winter vacation. Fiestas, bullfights, good food, and entertainment of every type are in store for all who make the short trip to *mañana* land.

Most tourists never become acquainted with any part of the city other than the three or four blocks near the border where the nightclubs and restaurants are located. However, like most American cities, it has its beautiful residential area and its poverty-stricken slum acres.

The east side has many expensive homes designed along ultra-modern lines, and the streets are broad and clean, while a short distance away is the section known as "Puebla Nueva," where thousands live in huts of adobe and straw and the streets are neither broad nor clean nor paved because the residents are too poor to own automobiles or pay taxes.

But these are only extremes. Actually, it is one of the most rapidly growing cities in Mexico. It is the gateway to the Mexicali Valley, which stretches from Laguna Salada nearly 130 miles southeast between the rugged Sierra del Capirote range and the Colorado River delta country to the famous fishing grounds of San Felipe on the Gulf of California. In 1930 the population of the entire valley was only 48,327. In 1950 it had jumped to 224,333.

To meet these population increases, Mexicali continued to improve its electrical and sewerage facilities. A roadbuilding program had been underway for years, and in 1950 a two-lane asphalt highway connecting San Felipe with Mexicali was completed.

No passports or visas were needed for Americans traveling across the border for periods not to exceed seventy-two hours. The Mexican people had extended a hand of welcome. Every week hundreds of southern California anglers poured across the international boundary along this new road to try their luck in the abundant waters of the Gulf.

It was the only route south that lay open to Cook.

Shortly after daylight, Deputy Waldrip, with Sheriff Ware and El Centro's chief of police, Guy Woodward, passed through Mexicali and drove toward San Felipe. In mid-afternoon, a few miles from the sleepy little village, they came upon a blue Buick sedan, headed north, parked on the right side of the highway. The rifles were gone, and the license plates were missing. But various items of camping equipment were strewn about inside, and the metal foot locker on the back seat was stamped "Dewey."

The tank still contained plenty of gas, but the hood was unlatched. The car apparently had developed motor trouble.

Three sets of footprints were visible in the sand alongside the car, and tire tracks indicated that another automobile had backed down the road to within thirty feet of the abandoned vehicle.

Soon FBI agents and Mexican police officials were pouring over the scene. They took samples of the bloodstains on the front cushion. They dusted for fingerprints, but found no clear patterns. They didn't need them. A maroon-colored sport shirt in the front seat was identified by Waldrip as a garment worn by his kidnapper when he had last seen him.

They made plaster casts of the footprints in the sand and photographed the tracks of the other automobile. There was no sign of skidding or spinning of the wheels. It had come to a stop, much as had Dewey's car on the desert stretch north of Ogilby.

Chief Woodward observed that the tracks had been made by the smallest-size tires commonly used on a passenger car—possibly a Ford, Plymouth, or Chevrolet.

From the different sizes of footprints—and one set obviously was Cook's—at least two men had given the killer a lift.

Realizing that these unwary motorists might be the next to die, the Mexican territorial police and FBI turned the Lower California peninsula into an armed zone and extended the roadblocks on both sides of the international boundary to Tijuana and the Pacific Ocean.

Since the abandoned car was headed north, the officers theorized Cook had found himself at a dead end at San Felipe, and realizing he was in a pocket, doubled back toward the border. They were determined to intercept him if he attempted to reenter the United States.

Cook didn't recross the border, and two men—Forrest Damron, 32, and his friend James Burke, 33—employees of a wholesale grocery firm in El Centro, were reported missing. Both men were amateur prospectors. They had left home on a trip to the Chocolate Mountains Friday night after telling their wives they would be back Sunday. They had not been heard from since.

"They've never stayed away like this before," Mrs. Burke told Sheriff Ware late Sunday night. "My husband and his friend were desert-bred and couldn't have got lost. We're afraid something else has happened."

Mrs. Damron had called her, she explained, and was "greatly worried."

Ware was well acquainted with Damron and Burke. Both were sons of prominent El Centro families and World War II veterans. Their wives were employed by Imperial County.

He figured the two men would have reached the mountains before Cook made his appearance in that section, and there was no evidence linking them with the squat, curly-haired marauder's flight to the border after slaying Dewey and taking his automobile.

"They are probably stalled someplace," the sheriff suggested, reassuringly. "Dozens of persons get stuck up in that country every year and we have to go after them."

Mrs. Burke protested. "They were driving my husband's new 1950 maroon Studebaker sedan, California license 86A2351. If the car became stalled, they would have walked to the nearest road and made their way back on foot. They know the country well, and know how to take care of themselves."

Ware promised to check. An extensive search of the area by air on Monday, and a combination ground and air search Tuesday were unsuccessful. On Wednesday, January 10, a posse of FBI agents and Imperial County deputies checking the San Felipe area for Cook learned that the missing men had been seen in the little fishing village Saturday night.

Residents told the posse men, "That's Burke," when shown photographs of the missing prospectors.

After leaving home Friday, the men apparently had changed their plans and gone to San Felipe.

There was no proof that their disappearance was connected with Cook. However, they could have been en route home Sunday afternoon, at the time the killer had abandoned Dewey's car on the highway.

With still no word from Damron and Burke by the end of the third day, it became increasingly certain that it was their car Cook had climbed into on the road to San Felipe.

Radio stations on both sides of the border broadcast descriptions of the missing men and their maroon Studebaker sedan in English and Spanish with a warning that Cook was heavily armed.

Three planes carrying FBI agents, Mexican police, and California highway patrol officers flew over key roads, distributing wanted flyers on Cook printed in Spanish.

At FBI headquarters in Washington, the fugitive desk handled a steady flow of teletype communications with field officers in the Southwest, seeing to it that they were well supplied with the posters.

They blanketed the country with nearly 100,000 notices, from Tijuana to the Colorado delta and the Mexican state of Sonora.

Two jeep parties led by FBI agents covered the roads to Kilometer 57 near the Sonora line. Five jeeps and one reconnaissance car led by an FBI agent covered the roads leading to Ensenada de Todos Santos. Another group of forty officers, ten cars, and eight horses covered the region of Colonia Zacatecas. Jeeploads of armed officers roamed the streets of the border towns. In Mexicali, one hundred Mexican police made a house-to-house check of the city.

At dawn Friday, with no sign of Cook and no word from Burke and Damron, the FBI announced that it was "highly probable" the killer had forced the two men to accompany him to the South District of the province from where Dewey's car was abandoned.

Within twenty-four hours, through Commandante Jesus V. Marroquin at Mexicali, the FBI arranged for a helicopter patrol of entire Lower California.

The helicopter patrol was coordinated with the ground searching parties in jeeps, reconnaissance cars, and on horseback. Jeeps and reconnaissance cars had to be used because automobiles could not stand the rough treatment of native roads, and the cat claw cactus would puncture an automobile tire like a sharp nail.

From the air, the terrain lay desolate and rugged to the extreme. Sand dunes and barren hummocks devoid of life, large drainage canals that criss-crossed them one mile apart, and hundreds of miles of giant saguaro cactus and underbrush, six feet in height, and forming a dense screen in which anything could be hidden, stretched to the sea. The maze of dusty, narrow roads, many of them nothing more than paths cut by wood-choppers through the wilderness, ran in crazy patterns and led no place in particular.

Every square mile of this country had to be searched. In a landscape such as this it wouldn't be too difficult for one man to hide from a large posse, particularly a criminally wise killer like Cook.

If he saw or heard a plane overhead, he could hide in a tree or the brush until it passed. He would make the most of resources at hand—live off the land or steal from others to keep up a day-to-day existence. If he had money, he might pay a native to hide him or, cold-blooded murderer that he was, take over one of the native shacks and kill all occupants.

Many were of the opinion that officers would "find several dead Mexicans" before they apprehended Cook.

In Imperial County, District Attorney Don Bitler charged the former Missouri juvenile delinquent with the murder of Robert Dewey, and announced that the state would attempt to send him to the gas chamber in San Quentin if he was captured alive and tried in

California. A federal charge was filed at San Diego accusing him of unlawful flight to avoid prosecution

In Oklahoma, Deputy Warren Smith filed five separate murder charges against Cook—one for each member of the Mosser family. Although no bodies had been found, Smith believed the charges would stand; that, on the basis of evidence uncovered thus far, the Mossers had been slain in Osage County.

At the same time, the FBI at Oklahoma City charged Cook with kidnapping under the seldom-used Lindbergh law.

The complaint, authorized by U.S. District Attorney Robert Shelton and filed before U.S. Commissioner Paul Showalter, accused Cook of transporting the Mosser family "in interstate commerce" from Oklahoma County to DeQueen, Arkansas, and "by force and violence, and to each, committed bodily harm, to wit: Murder."

It did not say, of course, where the murder might have occurred. It didn't have to.

The main body of the law reads: "Whoever knowingly transports in interstate or foreign commerce any person unlawfully seized, confined, inveigled, decoyed, kidnapped, abducted or carried away and held for ransom or reward or otherwise, except minors by parents, shall be punished by death if the kidnapped person has not been liberated unharmed and if the verdict of the jury shall so recommend or by imprisonment for any term of years or for life."

An added paragraph provides that if the kidnapped person is not released within seven days, a supposition is that the victim has been transported in interstate commerce, and the burden is placed on the defendant to prove otherwise.

That paragraph made possible the filing against Cook, even if actual evidence that he crossed state borders had not been in the government's hands.

The Lindbergh law grew out of the bizarre story of kidnapping, holding for ransom and killing of Charles Augustus Lindbergh, Jr., from his Hopewell, New Jersey, nursery, on March 1, 1932.

The case dragged on nearly four years before Bruno Richard Hauptmann, Bronx, New York, died in the New Jersey electric chair for killing the baby. He was tried and convicted under New Jersey statutes.

The original Lindbergh law enacted June 22, 1932, did not

provide a death penalty, only "imprisonment for any number of years or life at discretion of the court."

Some of the first life sentences were meted to members of the Barker-Karpis gang for the kidnapping on June 15, 1933, of William A. Hamm, Jr., wealthy brewer of St. Paul.

Little more than a month later, on July 22, 1933, Charles F. Urschel, Oklahoma City oilman, was kidnapped from his home. He was held nine days in a Texas farmhouse and released.

Seven persons were tried in Oklahoma City for kidnapping Urschel. George "Machine-gun" Kelly, his wife, Katherine, her parents, Mr. and Mrs. R. C. "Boss" Shannon, and Albert L. Bates and Harvey Bailey drew life terms.

On May 18, 1934, the law was amended to include the death penalty. The words "or otherwise" were inserted and kidnapping of children by parents was specifically excepted.

The first death penalty under the amended law was levied against Arthur Gooch. Gooch kidnapped two Paris, Texas, officers who were trying to arrest him in November 1934. His accomplice was Ambrose Nix.

Gooch and Nix took the officers into Pushmataha County, Oklahoma. The officers were freed and Nix was killed in the gun battle.

Gooch was found guilty of injuring one of the officers, and Federal District Judge R. L. Williams sentenced him to hang. The defense raised the "ransom or reward" issue and the case went to the U.S. Supreme Court, which upheld the district court.

Gooch was hanged on June 19, 1936, in the Oklahoma state penitentiary at McAlester. The scaffold had been built by the state at the cost of one dollar for the occasion.

In October 1950, the government had changed its mode of execution of death penalties to conform with that of the state in which the crime was committed. Should Cook be convicted of kidnapping the Mossers in Oklahoma, he would be electrocuted.

The armed robbery charge against him in the hijacking of Archer in Oklahoma County also carried the maximum penalty of death in the electric chair.

He now faced a four-way possibility of a death sentence.

If Damron and Burke had been killed in Lower California, he could still face another murder charge in the Mexican courts.

The families of the two men offered a reward of $500 for their discovery or the arrest of Cook. They posted the money with the American consulate in Mexicali.

As the FBI threw its full weight into the scope and intensity of the manhunt, Special Agent E. C. Richardson of the Southern California district at San Diego, set up temporary headquarters at El Centro, in the office of Sheriff Ware. More than a dozen agents had been assigned to the Imperial Valley alone, with at least fifty more combing the wilderness south of the border. It was the largest federal criminal operation since the days of John Dillinger, Pretty Boy Floyd, Clyde Barrow, and Bonnie Parker.

The blockade remained north of Cook. On one side was the broad Pacific and on the other the Gulf of California, both under heavy naval patrol. All fishing boats and ferries on which he might try to escape to the Mexican mainland were being closely watched. His pursuers pushed him steadily farther south, knowing that he was bound to run out of land.

It was like the calm before a storm. Peace officers play hunches, and for no explainable reason they believed the next forty-eight hours would tell the tale.

Meanwhile, they were riding with their hands on their guns. Most of them had children at home, and they intended to return alive.

Press associations reported that they were hunting Cook under orders to "shoot to kill," but Agent Richardson stated that such was not his instruction.

To the contrary, they wanted Cook alive so that he could be questioned regarding the location of the bodies of his first five victims.

CHAPTER 13

FIVE CORPSES IN A MURKY GRAVE

The war in Korea, politics, and taxes took a conversational back seat with extensive interest aroused in the missing Mosser family and the capture of their brutal slayer imminent. Everywhere people were asking themselves, "Where did Cook hide the bodies?"

Nobody knew for sure the exact route taken by the Missouri ex-con in his death-dealing ride. He had told Deputy Waldrip they were buried in the "snow in Oklahoma," but there had been no snow in the area he was believed to have traveled.

The bodies might be in a shallow grave off some lonely country lane. He might have hidden them in a ravine in the mountains of eastern Oklahoma or western Arkansas.

Or, as Deputy Warren Smith believed, they might be found in Osage County where the Mossers' bullet-punctured, blood-spattered vehicle had been abandoned.

Actually there was no way of knowing where they were and they might never be located unless Cook was captured alive.

The organized hunt for the family in Oklahoma ended after the systematic examination of all possible routes of their death trip failed to produce anything new. At sunset on Wednesday, January 10, highway patrol chief Norman Holt announced that his force was abandoning the search.

"This doesn't mean we won't keep trying," he said, "and we may keep a group in the Tulsa vicinity for another day or two. But all other troopers will be back on duty in their regular patrol districts."

It was a disappointing hour for the men. They had built hopes of finding the missing family.

Besides the lack of clues, two things made it difficult for the highway patrol to locate the bodies. One was the obviously warped personality of the murderer himself. Captain J. M. Thaxton, who had directed the hunt in the Henryetta-Okmulgee-Okemah area and southeastern part of the state, explained it this way:

"Cook's mode of operation is different from anything the troopers have encountered before. He's apparently hard clear through, with absolutely no regard for life. Usually, you'll find a soft spot somewhere in the way a man acts, but we haven't seen anything of that nature in this fellow.

"If you're following a bank robber, you can always try to figure out what you'd do under similar circumstances. But who in the world can warp his mind enough to place himself in the position of a man who'd kill a three-year-old child?"

He was referring to little Pamela Sue.

"Secondly, the troopers, because of their limited number, were forced to confine their search to highways and rural roads. Traveling slowly—and repeatedly climbing in and out of their cars—they looked under every bridge and culvert and through the bar ditches and some of the surrounding area.

"We cannot tramp through the woods, examine every farm pond, clump of bushes, or creek bed. And that's what it'll take. To make sure no spot is missed, it will take hundreds of people or even thousands. They will have to be organized and instructed not to destroy evidence.

"As of now," Thaxton concluded, "that is the only answer."

At Oklahoma City, Senator George Miskovsky and Representative J. D. McCarty introduced a joint resolution in both houses of the legislature to allow a special "quail day." The lawmakers believed that Oklahoma's thirty thousand quail hunters might turn up some sign of the family if allowed to loose their dogs in state fields for just one day. Quail season had closed the week before.

The senate passed the resolution and then rescinded it. They decided the quail hunting law could not be suspended by such action. It adopted, instead, a motion by Senator Louis Ritzhaupt, of Guthrie, asking Governor Johnston Murray for a proclamation calling on citizens to turn out in a wholehearted effort to find the bodies.

"I think it is a very commendable idea," Governor Murray said. "But we should go one step further."

He called Governor Sidney McMath at Little Rock. Governor McMath agreed to ask Arkansas citizens to do the same in his state.

They proclaimed Sunday, January 14, "Search Day for the Carl Mossers."

The plan was simple. In Oklahoma, Commissioner Gambill contacted the sheriffs of thirty-five eastern counties where it was believed the bodies might be hidden. He asked each sheriff to supervise the hunt in his own territory.

Each farmer and landowner was asked to make a detailed and careful search of his own property and any vacant property next to him. Farmers with large sections of land which they couldn't search themselves would call upon their sheriff for help. The sheriff, in turn, would furnish searchers from volunteers. All volunteers would report to the sheriffs of their respective counties.

Open range and state-owned land, public parks, and other similar areas would be worked by law enforcement officers and volunteers of the county in which they were located. State troopers would assist the sheriffs and volunteers in each patrol district.

"In that way the sheriff can arrange to cover every foot of ground in his county," Gambill said. "If those bodies are in Oklahoma, we should find them."

Herman Lindsey, director of the Arkansas State Police, planned a thorough search of ten counties stretching from DeQueen to the southern Missouri border. His force of troopers would be aided by local officers and fifteen radio-equipped units of the state fish and game commission. Residents of the remote mountainous areas would be asked to ride in the cars to point out secluded roads and trails.

Incentive to find the Carl Mossers mounted on Saturday as the Arkansas Sheriffs' Association, meeting in Fort Smith, offered a $100 reward to the person who found them in Arkansas. In Illinois, a similar fund, started by friends of the family at Atwood and Hammond, jumped to $1,700.

The mass hunt started Sunday at 7 A.M. And the worst weather of the season set in.

Planes scheduled to participate in the hunt were grounded. Searchers at Tulsa moved out in a blinding snowstorm. In Osage and adjoining counties, the hunt failed to materialize because of rain and driving snow.

Elsewhere, county roads became impassable. Police cars bogged down and had to be helped by others. Water-soaked roads hampered work in Creek County, and groups of volunteers hunted on horseback. In many localities, a day-long drizzling rain cut the number of volunteers to a minimum.

Despite these setbacks, hundreds of farmers combed the areas close to their homes. Thousands of officers and citizens fought through thickets, peered into old wells and deep gullies, sloshed through ponds and creeks, and dragged lakes and rivers.

Hopes of finding the family were bolstered for a time when a two-inch piece of flesh with some reddish-blond hair was found by a farmer's dog near Leach, in Delaware County. But it was analyzed by a Tulsa pathologist as "animal and definitely not human."

Shoes, shirts, bedclothes, and a bloodstained scarf were turned in at police departments and sheriffs' offices, and a stained, torn cotton dress, apparently owned by a child, was pulled from James Fork Creek by a game warden and deputy sheriff at Hackett, Arkansas. But none of these items belonged to the Mossers.

When the tired, soaked searchers returned to their homes at nightfall, the whereabouts of the Illinois farm family was as much an enigma as on January 3 when their automobile had been found near Tulsa.

One Tulsan created a flurry of excitement on Sunday night. W. L. Lawson reported to Criminal Deputy Lovelace that he and his son had found Carl Mosser's wallet just off the road, three hundred yards south of where the car had been abandoned.

"My boy and I had hunted that area before, but decided this afternoon to take another look," Lawson explained.

"The road was muddy, and I stepped over to the patch of grass to wipe my feet when I spotted the wallet."

How the wallet, filled with Mosser's papers and identification, had been overlooked by earlier searchers puzzled Lovelace.

He wondered if Cook had thrown it away after he hitched a ride to the Osage Hills shopping center on January 2.

Lovelace retraced the route from the point where the car was abandoned, and another deputy threw the wallet out unobstrusively as they figured Cook might have done. It landed within inches of where Lawson and his son had found it.

But Lloyd Edwards, who had given Cook the ride, could not recall the killer throwing anything out of his car. "I remember the window was up on the right side, and he didn't lower it or make any kind of move until I let him out at the drugstore."

The wallet undoubtedly had been in Cook's possession—the money was missing. So it couldn't have slipped from Mosser's pocket.

"Cook could have dropped it while removing the bodies from the car, then drove to the spot where he got stuck in the ditch," Edwards said.

This theory again glued attention of searchers for the missing family to the Osage Hills.

More significant was the disclosure of a Tulsa testing laboratory that soil samples taken from the mud-caked murder showed a heavy shale content. "It could have come from a refuse hill around an abandoned lead and zinc mine," technicians added.

The weather bureau reported snow flurries had occurred around Miami, Commerce, Quapaw, and Picher the night of January 1, and searchers began poking through refuse hills in northeastern Oklahoma mining country on the Kansas-Missouri border.

The giant piles of gravel, sand, and waste material from old mine diggings surround deep craters, like they say might be found on the moon. They give the land an eerie appearance of a strange planet in outer space. Light in color, they resemble snowbanks at night. They groan under their own shifting weight. A slit pressure would start a slide on these shale mounds that could easily have buried five persons. Cook could have re-entered Oklahoma in the Joplin area and driven through Quapaw and Miami before killing his victims.

Chief Carl Nutt and Detective Gamble, at Joplin, believed that Cook had driven up the western edge of Arkansas, after being seen with the Mossers at Winthrop, and back to the mine-punctured area that had spawned him. As a boy, he had played about the abandoned lead and zinc mines of Chitwood, only four blocks north of U.S. 66. He knew every nook and crevice. It was nearly 300 miles from Winthrop to Joplin, and 139 miles from Joplin to Tulsa, which would come closer to accounting for the additional 600 miles on the Mosser vehicle.

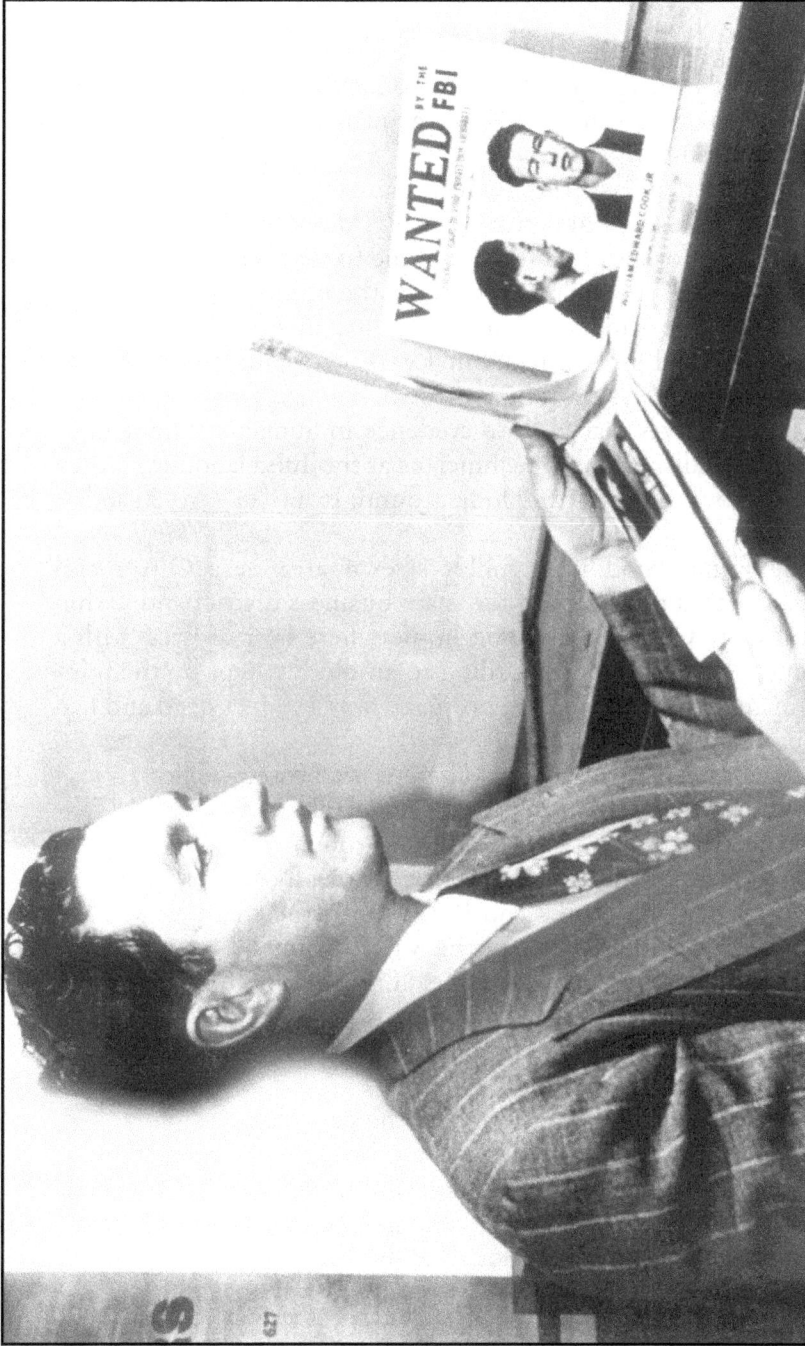

Chief of Detectives Carl Nutt, of Joplin, Missouri, examines Cook's criminal record. Chief Nutt led the search of the rubble-strewn mining area just west of Joplin's business district that led to the discovery of the bodies of the Mosser family in a 110-foot-deep abandoned mine shaft.

Working round-the-clock with the FBI in an effort to close all gaps in Cook's background, Nutt and Gamble learned that he had threatened to shoot an ex-convict acquaintance and throw him down a hundred-foot shaft.

"It happened last July," Gene Suman told the detectives. "Right after Bill came home from prison. I'd known Bill a long time before in the reformatory. He wanted me to join him in a hijacking career. When I refused, he forced me at the point of a gun to walk to this shaft. He threatened to throw me in unless I gave him money. I only had two dollars, but I gave it to him, and he let me go. I hid out two days until he left town."

The detectives placed little credence in Suman's statement at first. After the disclosure of technicians at the Tulsa laboratory, they decided to go to the shaft and look around. It was 11 A.M., Monday, January 15.

The mine stood in a rubble-strewn area near Oliver and Second streets, a mile west of the main business district and within two blocks of Cook's childhood home where he had lived with a foster mother. The shaft, according to an old log kept by the mining company which owned the property, was 110 feet deep and had been abandoned for years.

It was cemented at the top. There was a protective floor about six feet square built of fourteen two-inch planks laid over three railroad ties to keep livestock from falling through.

Two pieces of the flooring had been torn loose!

Nutt lifted the planks and looked into the shaft. It was too dark to clearly see the surface of the water thirty feet below. "Bring the searchlight," he called to Gamble. "I think something is floating around down there."

The searchlight's powerful beams cut the darkness and played onto a body.

The beams caught another body, then another.

A call to the Joplin fire department brought emergency rescue equipment. They rigged a three-foot-square wooden raft to a steel cable on a winch truck. Then a veteran fireman named Henry T. Cook, who spat at the mention that he might be related to the killer, slipped an air mask over his head and was lowered into the depth. He found a pile of timber choking the shaft. Floating above the timbers in the murky water were five bodies.

Crowd of people from Joplin at abandoned mine site where Cook disposed of his murder victims.

Bodies of five of Cook's victims—Carl and Thelma Mosser and their three children—recovered from the abandoned Missouri mine.

The fireman handled them gently. He signaled and the cable pulled him to the surface. He was holding Pamela Sue.

Next came Gary Carl, then Ronald Dean, then the mother, and finally the father.

Pamela Sue and Gary Carl had been shot through the heart. Powder burns indicated the killer had held the gun at less than arm's length, possibly while they struggled in his grip.

Ronald Dean had been shot three times, twice through the heart and once in the head. He was gagged and his wrists bound with a yellow cord torn from his cowboy hat, a Christmas gift he had insisted on wearing to visit his Uncle Chris in Albuquerque.

Thelma Mosser's hands were tied tightly behind her back and a piece of Turkish towel stuffed in her throat. She had been shot through the chest.

Mosser had been shot once, in the head. He was gagged, but the bonds on his wrists were loose. Obviously he had tried to free himself in a desperate effort to save his family.

Blood had trickled over another of Ronald Dean's prize possessions—a wallet stamped "Hopalong Cassidy" which still contained a dollar bill, six dimes, and fifteen pennies, the only money Cook had not taken from his victims.

Hundreds of spectators jammed the streets leading to the mine after news of the discovery spread. Folks don't shock easily in Chitwood and adjoining Smelter Hill. They have seen plenty of life in the raw. But they stood dazed and aghast as firemen and volunteer workers carefully laid the bodies of the Mossers side by side on a tarpaulin spread over the barren ground.

Old Will Cook, appearing briefly on the scene, said, "God help Bill for doing anything like this. It's sure awful, ain't it?"

An angry rumble rose from the restless crowd as the girl was stretched out on the piece of canvas.

Dr. W. W. Hurst, coroner, made his preliminary examination and expressed an opinion that all five had been slain in Jasper County. "They were dead only a short time before being dumped into the water."

Lieutenant Chris Mosser arrived from Tulsa with two police detectives. He nearly collapsed after viewing the bodies.

"I'm glad it's over," said Chris as he bit into his lips. "It has been hell these past two weeks—knowing they were dead but dreading to find out how they died. If they had to die at the hands of this beast, thank the Lord he killed them without torturing them."

Afterward, the bodies were removed to a funeral home in Joplin. The grim task, begun at 11:55 A.M., was over in less than an hour.

At the same moment, even as the angry rumble rose from the crowd that stood and watched the fireman struggle from the shaft bearing his first horrible burden, officers in Mexico were closing in on the stocky, thick-lipped youth who had grown up in their midst.

CHAPTER 14
CAPTURE AT SANTA ROSALIA

From Xavier Gonzales, paymaster of a silver mine halfway down the peninsula, came word that on Tuesday, January 9, he had passed a maroon sedan on a narrow stretch of road in the hills near El Marmal and exchanged greetings with three men.

"They were Americans," Gonzales told Police Chief Kraus Morales of Tijuana.

Chief Morales and his men were working one end of the "pincer movement" along the single highway leading into the South District through the Sierra de Santa Catarina mountains.

A cryptic piece of advice appears on maps of the sparsely populated, desolate region: "Do not start over any earth road shown here without first making exhaustive local inquiry as to its condition and securing the services of a competent guide." The highway runs south five hundred miles to the Gulf and Santa Rosalia. From there a ferry steamer plied the Gulf of Guaymas, on the Mexican mainland.

"The men claimed to be hunters," Gonzales added. He had noticed the lack of camping equipment in the car, but thought nothing of it at the time. Upon leaving the hills Saturday, he had seen the flyer with Cook's photograph. "The man in the back seat was Cook. They were headed for El Marmal."

While the officers in their radio-equipped jeeps continued to work down the narrow slip of land, Chief Morales left by plane for El Marmal.

He showed residents of the half-abandoned mining village Cook's photograph.

"*Sí*, the man was here. But he left a few days ago," they said.

Chief Morales continued south sixty miles to Puerto Prieta. He got the same story.

The next stop was Santa Rosalia. Morales arrived the morning of January 15. He went to Chief of Police Parra Rodriguez.

"If Cook is in Rosalia, we will find him," Rodriguez promised.

They started out in a patrol wagon to cover the main street of the wind-blown city.

While riding eastward, halfway along the street, they spotted three Americans—two dressed in hunting clothes, the third wearing a leather windbreaker.

They drove past them slowly and stopped around the next corner. The two chiefs got out, and hurried back along the street. The three men had entered a restaurant.

They glanced through the plate-glass window. The trio were seated in a booth near the entrance. The two in hunting attire faced them, the third sat with his back to the door.

The officers stepped inside and moved quickly up to the booth. Rodriguez placed the muzzle of his .45 service pistol against the nape of Cook's neck and told him to stand up. With his left hand he pulled a .38 revolver from Cook's belt, handed it to Chief Morales, and took a .32 pistol from Cook's jacket pocket. He ordered all three men to stand against the wall and searched them. Then Chief Morales handcuffed Cook.

It was 12:02 P.M., Pacific time, when the arrest was made and the manhunt across two countries ended.

The men with the fugitive identified themselves as Forrest Damron and James Burke. At headquarters, Damron told how they had seen Cook standing beside an automobile north of San Felipe on Sunday, January 7. "He seemed to be in trouble and we stopped to give him a lift. He got in the back seat, but it wasn't until we heard a wanted bulletin for him on our car radio that he drew his gun.

"He put the .38 in my face, and I told Jim, 'You'd better look around. I think we're in grave trouble.'"

Cook had ordered Burke to keep both hands on the wheel, and Damron to put his arms up where they could be seen. As Damron turned to place his arms on the dash, one of them slipped from sight momentarily, which startled Cook. He pulled the trigger at Damron's head, but the hammer fell on a spent cartridge.

Cook quickly spun the cylinder and said, "It will work next time."

He made them return to the Buick, Damron related, where he loaded two rifles wrapped in a blanket into their car.

"Next he asked for our wallets, taking Jim's first, mine second. He took our money and kept Jim's identification cards and registration papers on the car. He told us he was going over into Old Mexico, dispose of the automobile, and remain there on the money, and that from here on he was Jim Burke, and if we didn't do as he said, he'd kill us and dump our bodies into the Gulf.

"We started over the mountains, but he didn't like Jim's driving. He cursed him and made him stop the car and told me to take the wheel. At that time he noticed Jim was wearing a red shirt and ordered him to keep his jacket zipped. When we asked him why, he told us that he was last seen wearing a red shirt. He seemed to think Jim's shirt would get him identified."

Then, for a fantastic week, they had been his prisoners while Cook sat behind them, like an alert cat, his hands never more than inches from the butt of the revolver tucked in his belt.

They drove by day and slept at night, sitting in the front seat, wrapped in blankets with their arms pinioned, while Cook dozed in the back with a gun in his lap. If they needed to relieve themselves, they asked Cook.

They never could tell when he was asleep or awake because of his "peculiar eye." He warned them never to move while they thought he was asleep. They always spoke to him in the morning when they awoke before making a move.

"We weren't about to do anything foolish," explained Damron.

Cook already had told them there had been eight passengers in three other cars he had ridden in, and that all eight of them were dead.

"We ate on the beaches," Burke said, "building campfires and heating dried foods and jerky meat that we picked up along the way—never twice in the same place. He insisted that we act like friends. He even let us do some target shooting with one of the rifles, firing into the seaside cliffs along the way, so the natives would think we were just on an outing. But all the time he had the revolver in his hand, and warned he would kill us if we tried to turn the rifle on him.

"This morning we wanted to come into town—Santa Rosalie—to get something to eat. Cook didn't want to come.

"Damron said, 'I'd like some of those native oranges.' We'd ate some before.

"Cook asked, 'Do you think we could find some?'

"We assured him we could, and it was the luckiest thing we ever did!

"We're mighty grateful to you officers," Burke concluded. "You saved our lives."

Morales and Rodriguez flew the heavily manacled prisoner to Tijuana, where he was ordered deported as an undesirable alien. A few minutes later, they escorted Cook from the Tijuana police station and thrust him across the international boundary into the waiting hands of the FBI. He was lodged in jail at San Diego.

Questioned by FBI chief Richardson and his agents, Cook pleaded a complete memory blackout. He had got drunk in Blythe on Christmas day and woke up in the desert fifty miles south of Mexicali with a broken-down car and a gun in his hand.

"I tried to get the car started, but I couldn't. Then two men came along and gave me a ride. They saw my gun and started driving south. They didn't try to get away. They acted scared of me.

"I heard on their car radio that I was wanted and officers had been instructed to 'shoot to kill' if they found me. They said I had killed some family."

He was stolid and unmoved when told that the bodies of his five victims had been found in an abandoned mine shaft. "I'm a good boy!" he said sullenly. "I never killed anybody! All those reports are false!"

Cook was arraigned before U.S. Commissioner George Baird on Monday afternoon. Baird fixed bail at $25,000 on each of the unlawful flight counts, but denied bail on the kidnapping charge and set his preliminary hearing for January 29.

On Tuesday, the questioning of FBI agents continued. Cook sat at a desk in one of the conference rooms at the San Diego

County jail. A stream of sunlight struck his face through a nearby window. He stared at the floor in front of him with his right hand supporting his forehead.

When he replied at all, it was in a barely audible monotone.

Asked directly if he had ever kidnapped or killed anybody, he said, "I don't remember."

"Do you remember Homer Waldrip?"

"No."

"Do you remember Robert Dewey?"

"No."

Richardson asked, "Why do you suppose they have charged you with these crimes?"

Cook merely shook his head.

"Why did they settle on you?" another agent, Henry Plaxico, asked.

"I don't know."

"Why did you shoot the oldest Mosser boy three times?" asked Plaxico. "Did he fight with you in an attempt to protect his mother and his dad and his brother and sister?"

"I never knew anybody named Mosser," came the poker-faced denial in a whisper-like voice.

"Were the little kids scared when you started shooting that night in the car?" asked Plaxico. "Did they scream and try to break loose when you held them in your arms and shot them?"

"I don't remember anything."

"Why did you drive all the way to Texas and over into Arkansas before you killed the Mossers? When did you decide that the old mine shaft in Joplin would be a good place to hide the bodies?"

"I don't know what you are talking about or why you are asking me all these questions," the stocky gunman mumbled.

"How did you feel when your dad left you and your sisters and brother in that cave in Joplin when you were a child?"

"I don't remember," said Cook. Then he appeared to take an interest in the one-sided conversation. He added: "I don't mean anything to my father."

Asked if his father wasn't his friend and hadn't tried to keep him out of trouble, he said, "I never had a friend in all my life. Nobody ever liked me and they never will. Nobody ever did anything for me. They always did things to me.

"They sent me to a reform school when I was eleven. There they beat me. They used a rubber hose and beat me all the time. Then I went to the penitentiary. There was a bunch of dumb guards—they couldn't even read—beat me on the head every time they saw me. They were rough and mean, always mean as hell."

Then he lapsed back to sullen silence.

The only time Cook looked up during the interrogation was when Richardson offered him a cigarette. He either did not hear the offer at first or he simply ignored it.

"Would you like a cigarette?" Richardson asked. "I didn't hear what you said."

He raised his eyes, looked directly at the FBI chief and shook his head.

"You do smoke, don't you?"

That brought only a nod.

Tuesday night the gruesome details of the brutal murder of six persons remained a secret—locked behind the cruel, thick lips of the Joplin badman.

Meanwhile, R. M. Zimmers, FBI ballistics expert in the bureau's Washington laboratory, identified Cook's .32 automatic as the gun used to kill the Mossers. The serial number showed it to be the same weapon Cook had purchased in El Paso. The scientific examination further showed that two bullets removed from Dewey's body had been fired from Deputy Waldrip's .38 revolver, recovered from the gunman at the time of his capture.

Faced with this evidence, Cook became more tractable, and from his lips came the story of his senseless, bloody rampage. Of the slaying of the Mossers, he said: "The kids were crying, the dame was hysterical and started screaming. It was too risky. I didn't want them to get the cops on me, so I plugged them all!"

Agent Plaxico took the badman's statement.

Cook and the Mossers had arrived at the outskirts of Joplin and stopped in a vacant field off the highway pursuant to an agreement with the family that he was to leave them bound and gagged in the car in order that he would have time to escape.

Then came the tragic incident that resulted in their deaths.

Cook was in the process of binding his victims when a police car passed and two officers looked them over carefully and drove on. As the tail lights of the police car faded away, the woman and children began screaming, so he shot the entire family.

Cook then slid under the wheel, drove to the abandoned mine and dumped the bodies into the shaft. He placed the time at 3 A.M.

That ended three days of terror for the Mossers—three nightmarish days spent with Cook's gun trained on them while they traveled almost aimlessly through Oklahoma, Texas, New Mexico, and Arkansas.

It began on December 30, when he stopped the family after hijacking Archer, and with his gun forced entry into their car. "I was a little excited—thought the cops were after me—and left my things in the Buick convertible. I told the man to drive to Oklahoma City, and if they did as I said they would not get hurt."

They finally arrived at Oklahoma City, rode around town for "about an hour," then drove to Wichita Falls, where they bought gasoline at the small grocery-service station.

Cook told the FBI agents that Mosser "tried to escape here," but he did not elaborate on the incident.

He then went on to describe how he forced Mosser to drive as far west as Carlsbad, New Mexico, then south to El Paso. Here Cook became frightened when a police car got "too close for comfort," and ordered Mosser to "turn around and head eastward."

They drove to Houston, Texas. From Houston, they proceeded to Winthrop, Arkansas, where Mosser bought some food for the family.

"Then we drove to Fort Smith and north to Joplin, where I killed them."

In making the statement, Cook showed no remorse and offered no other excuse than that he feared apprehension.

After disposing of the bodies, he drove to Tulsa. "I arrived in the morning as people were going to work. I was excited and didn't want to be seen with all that blood in the car. I swung off on a side street and headed west on a dirt road. I slid into a muddy ditch and had to leave the car."

He had left Tulsa by bus, and by combining short trips with random hitchhikes, had worked his way back to Blythe and "run into Waldrip" at the motel.

He hadn't actually "killed seven."

"I was only boasting to Waldrip. He was supposed to be number six. I don't know why I changed my mind."

Describing the murder of Dewey, he said, "I turned on the red flasher light, and he stopped his car.

"I said, 'You've got yourself in a pretty bad jam, haven't you, fellow?' He said, 'No, not that I know of.'

"Yes, you did—you ran over a little girl two miles down the road and you didn't stop.

"I got in the car and told him to drive back to where he hit the girl. He was very nervous and asked if he could smoke a cigarette. I told him to go ahead—he dropped it between the seat and front door—and when he reached for it, I thought I heard a click, and shot him in the side with the deputy's revolver. He looked around kind of startled and said, 'You can't scare me, I've been shot before,' and then lunged at me, fumbling with the door handle at the same time. The door came open, and as he slumped out into the road, I shot him again and slid over under the wheel. I guess he didn't have a gun after all. If he hadn't got nervous and made the move he did, he would still be alive."

After signing the confession, Cook looked up at Plaxico and asked, "How high do they hang you in Oklahoma?"

"Pretty high," the agent replied, and Cook said, "I guess all I can do now is act crazy and get the sympathy of the people."

At the same moment, two hundred persons crowded the little chapel in Atwood, Illinois, for the funeral services of the Carl Mosser family. A public address system was set up to bring the services to hundreds more who stood outside.

More than five hundred filed past the five gray caskets holding the bodies of Mosser, his wife Thelma, and their three children—Ronald Dean, Gary Carl and Pamela Sue. Afterward, the bodies were taken eight miles to the Hammond, Illinois, cemetery and lowered into graves covering two cemetery lots.

At the farm north of Atwood that Carl Mosser rented, a waiting Collie dog and Christmas wreaths still hanging on doors and windows were stirring reminders of a whole family wiped out by the gun of a brutal desperado.

CHAPTER 15

"THE DAMNEDEST TRAVESTY ON JUSTICE EVER"

Cook's confession served to strengthen the kidnapping charge against him in Oklahoma. Venue in such cases lies in the federal district where the crime has its beginning.

U.S. District Attorney Robert E. Shelton air-mailed a certified copy of the arrest warrant for the multiple killer to U.S. District Attorney Ernest Tolin in Los Angeles.

"The crime was committed in the western Oklahoma district when he kidnapped the Mossers near Luther," explained Shelton. "We know he took them into Texas and Arkansas, and we know their bodies were found in Missouri. It makes no difference where the family died, the crime was in kidnapping and taking the members, while they were alive, across state lines."

He requested that Cook be returned to Oklahoma, and asked U.S. District Judge Stephen S. Chandler to issue a grand jury call.

"I will ask this grand jury to indict Cook and bring him to trial immediately," Shelton added.

District Attorney Don Bitler, of Imperial County, spoke about Cook's custody. "I will not battle the federal government," Bitler stated. "He should be tried where they have the strongest case. We have an excellent case against him in California for the murder of Robert Dewey. We also have him charged with the armed robbery of Waldrip. If it's charges they want, we can charge him with kidnapping Waldrip, robbing Dewey, and stealing two automobiles."

He was referring to five separate Mosser murder charges filed against Cook by the Jasper County, Missouri, prosecuting attorney, Dave Tourtelot, at Joplin. But Tourtelot said, "We regard these merely as insurance to be invoked if the federal case falls short of the death penalty."

"We intend to do everything possible to send Cook to the electric chair in the Oklahoma state penitentiary at McAlester," Shelton assured them. "We've asked for him. We're going to try to get him. I think we can make our case."

In San Diego, Cook refused to eat, talk with officials, or waive his preliminary hearing set for January 29. In Oklahoma City, Shelton pressed for an indictment.

"An indictment here will make the preliminary hearing in California unnecessary," he announced. "Cook could waive the preliminary hearing and the removal hearing and be transferred to this federal district at once. A removal hearing cannot be held without a preliminary, but they can be held at the same time. But if Cook is indicted here, a removal hearing can be held at once because the preliminary has become a moot question.

"I've done everything I can to speed up the trial. The next move is Cook's. I'm sitting here tapping my foot, waiting."

Ray H. Kinnison, chief of the criminal division of the U.S. attorney's office at Los Angeles, went to San Diego at once. He simply informed Cook that he could sign a waiver, or prepare for the preliminary hearing as scheduled, and asked if he had employed a lawyer.

"I've only got fifty dollars and I don't think it would do any good to hire a lawyer here," Cook replied.

The rest was a mere formality. He was arraigned in his jail cell Thursday. U.S. Commissioner Baird asked if he was willing to waive removal hearing. Cook replied, "I'll sign a waiver."

With his hands and feet shackled, the prisoner was taken by automobile under heavy guard to Los Angeles and put aboard a train to Oklahoma.

He arrived in Oklahoma City at 1:27 P.M., Sunday, January 21, shackled to two deputy U.S. marshals. The former juvenile delinquent cringed as he walked between rows of plainclothes men and uniformed officers who held back a huge crowd at Union Station.

There was no shouting. The crowd merely watched him pass and discussed his crimes in hushed tones.

"He can't look you in the face," one woman said.

"Someone ought to kill him now and save the government the expense of going to trial," a young man told his wife.

He was whisked into a waiting sedan and taken to the county courthouse behind the screeching sirens of a motorcycle escort. Another crowd saw him enter the jail.

The federal grand jury convened on Tuesday, January 23. Before impaneling the jury, Judge Chandler had the confessed killer brought to court.

Cook maintained an air of stony melancholy during the brief appearance. He stared at the floor and spoke only those few words which were necessary, but politely said "sir" when addressing the black-robed judge.

Chandler asked if he could afford a lawyer.

"If you can hire one for about fifty dollars, I can," Cook replied.

"Under the circumstances, I think it is my duty to appoint an attorney to defend you," Chandler said. He had called Gomer Smith and John Connolly, prominent Oklahoma City attorneys, into the courtroom to witness the proceedings.

"It is the duty of a lawyer, when appointed to serve without compensation, to represent his client to the best of his ability and to protect his legal rights," Chandler continued. "These men are good lawyers and will represent you well."

Both attorneys had been active in Democratic party politics in Oklahoma for many years. They had large law practices, but if they were unhappy about being named to defend the notorious Cook, they carefully hid their feelings. A dozen Oklahoma City attorneys, interviewed by reporters before Cook's return, had agreed they didn't want his case.

"It appears hopeless," they said.

Smith and Connolly held a fifteen-minute conference with their client. But Cook would give them nothing coherent or helpful. They asked Shelton not to call Cook before the grand jury, and pointed out, "He is not required to appear if he objects."

"His testimony will not be necessary to get the indictment," Shelton quipped.

He had Cook placed in the U.S. marshal's detention in the federal building. After witnesses from four states, waiting to testify before the grand jury, filed past to look at him, he was escorted back to the county jail.

Lloyd Edwards of Tulsa viewed Cook and said, "He's the man."

Rancher Pete Essley also identified him.

But E. O. Cornwell of Wichita Falls didn't believe he was one of the two men he had chased from his station the night of December 30: "The man was about Cook's size, but he doesn't look like him."

Lee Burd Archer of Tahoka, Texas, identified Cook without hesitation. "That's the man. I was with him ten hours. I'd know him anywhere."

Mrs. Rufus Smith of Winthrop, Arkansas, was positive he was the man with Mosser when the Atwood, Illinois, farmer bought sandwiches and coffee from her on January 1.

Ninety minutes of expectant death flashed back in thirty seconds when Deputy Sheriff Homer Waldrip looked through the bars at his erstwhile kidnapper.

"Hello, Bill," he said in a low voice.

Cook's droopy eye raised a trifle as he glanced at the man he told he was going to make his eighth death victim.

"Don't you know this fellow?" one of the deputy marshals asked.

"I've never seen him before," Cook muttered.

Waldrip turned and walked away. "He remembers me all right," the deputy said, "and I sure remember him."

Judge Chandler made no mention of the Mosser case as he impaneled the jury. But he cautioned, "Do not permit public clamor to influence your actions."

The jury indicted Cook as soon as the witnesses completed their testimony.

On Thursday, January 25, the prisoner was whisked from the county jail to the federal building by deputy marshals at 7 A.M. to avoid curious spectators. Judge Chandler's courtroom was filled long before the arraignment began at 9:15.

Cook wore khaki pants, a leather jacket and blue shirt open at the neck. He stood stone-faced and rigid, and spoke less than a dozen words to his lawyers before Judge Chandler took the bench.

Chandler asked the district attorney to read the indictment. As Shelton began reading the lengthy document, Connolly interrupted and announced that Cook was ready to make a "not guilty plea."

Chandler asked Cook, "Do you know what you are charged with?"

Cook hesitated, then mumbled, "Kidnapping."

Connolly entered the plea of innocence, and Judge Chandler ordered him held for trial without bond. Then Gomer Smith addressed the court.

"This man already has had an *ex parte* trial. The district attorney has announced the date of the indictment, the outcome of the arraignment, and the public at large has decided everything else except the date he is to be executed.

"Would your honor please explain to this man that we are his attorneys and do not represent the government? When you stated we were officers of the court, he decided we were just another pair of federal agents and has refused to cooperate with us at all.

"If this apparent hostility continues, we can only ask for permission to withdraw. Please tell him we have been appointed to help save him and not to kill him."

Cook's expression never changed. He stood with his arms folded behind him, staring at the floor.

"In this country," Judge Chandler told Cook, "if a man cannot afford to hire counsel, then it is up to the court to appoint counsel for him. These men are officers of the court but they are *your* lawyers. They understand, as does the court, the seriousness of the crime with which you are charged. They owe you a debt and they cannot represent the government.

"The government is represented by the district attorney and his staff. My duty is to see that you get a fair trial, *and you will get a fair trial.*

"You have certain constitutional rights guaranteed by the Constitution of the United States and those constitutional rights will be preserved for you.

"These men are serving you without pay but that will not lessen their zeal to defend you well. The court was careful to appoint capable and competent lawyers to defend you. You are making a great mistake if you do not cooperate with them."

Cook barely glanced at Judge Chandler while he spoke. Heavily armed marshals stood around the walls of the courtroom. Another deputy stood behind Cook.

"Are you satisfied with your lawyers?" the judge asked. "If you aren't, I will appoint someone else to take your case."

With that Cook raised his head level with Judge Chandler's eyes and mumbled, "I guess so."

The defense lawyers maintained they would need at least six weeks to prepare for trial.

"Ours may be a defense that the average layman may not understand," Smith stated, without elaborating. "We have a lot of witnesses to interview, a lot of places to go."

Shelton thought it could be done in three weeks.

Judge Chandler consulted his calendar and set the trial for March 26.

The arraignment over, Cook's attorneys asked that he be taken to the marshal's office where they could talk with him. When they emerged a few minutes later, Connolly announced to reporters: "Cook will not help us perfect his defense."

Then, on March 13, in a surprise move seeking to beat the electric chair, Cook switched his innocent plea to guilty while his attorneys sought to establish that he was insane.

Gomer Smith told Judge Chandler, "We have no defense to the things Cook is charged with. All we can do is present the mitigating circumstances, point out his mental infirmities that make it impossible, under the criminal code, for him to be guilty of kidnapping and murder."

Shelton protested. "I will insist on a jury trial. It is my understanding that under the Lindbergh law only a jury can assess the death penalty."

Judge Chandler quoted a recent decision in which the U.S. Circuit Court of Appeals at Denver had ruled that, when a jury trial is waived by the defendant, sentence of the court carries the same weight as a jury verdict. "In this case the judge had a legal right to assess life imprisonment after the defendant had pleaded guilty to murder."

Shelton observed, "The circuit court might be inclined to regard a death penalty levied by a lone judge in a different light." Then added: "I can recall not one instance where a federal judge has levied a death sentence without a jury."

"The mitigating circumstances, life and background mental infirmities of the defendant are such as to preclude a death sentence," Smith argued.

"We have entered a plea of guilty to eliminate a long trial and the tremendous expense. And to get away from Roman holiday atmosphere. Let's not have a Roman holiday with this boy. The Roman holiday atmosphere where prisoners were thrown to the lions for enjoyment of the populace is not a fine reflection on civilization."

"As to the expense involved," replied Shelton, "it has already cost society and the taxpayer in general an estimated $500,000 to apprehend Cook. Why worry about it now?"

Cook stood with his eyes closed. His folded hands showed the word "HARD" tattooed across his fingers. He barely lifted his voice above a whisper when he answered "Guilty" to each of the five counts of kidnapping.

Then Smith told Judge Chandler, "It is the responsibility of the court to sentence this defendant. A jury is only advisory and in the final analysis the court must fix the punishment."

Chandler replied that he knew the full responsibility rested on him. "I myself can render the death verdict." The judge did not indicate whether there would be a jury trial. He merely said, "I want to be sure Cook is mentally competent to enter a plea. I will accept the plea, but I can force him to withdraw it if I find him mentally incompetent." He ordered a sanity hearing for March 20.

Three Oklahoma City psychiatrists—Dr. James H. Parker, chief of the Veterans Administration's regional neuropsychiatric department; Dr. Waymon Thompson, federal jail physician; and Dr. Moorman Prosser—testified for the prosecution. Three psychologists, Dr. Milton Wechsler, Dr. Donald Watterson and Martin Maymond, of the Menninger clinic in Topeka, Kansas, and Dr. Hugh Galbraith, Oklahoma City psychiatrist, appeared for the defense.

Dr. Galbraith stated, in his opinion, Cook "is among the worst" compared with backward patients in any state mental hospital. "I doubt if he would commit suicide, but he might rig a deal so he could be killed."

Galbraith had "spent nearly six hours" with the slayer and Cook answered his questions, although he sometimes had to "pry" the answers from him.

He related portions of Cook's background, the "unhealthful influences," particularly the droopy eyelid that had given him a peculiar appearance throughout life, the death of his mother when he was five, his life as a "boarded-out" child, his trips to the state reformatory and eventual conviction for armed robbery.

"He has the emotional reaction of a child of 3. He is incapable of assisting his lawyers in his own defense. He is incapable of making plans. He lives in a world of his own. His severe mental illness will make him dangerous for years to come. Patients like this are kept in hospitals indefinitely," Dr. Galbraith concluded.

In answer to a direct question by Gomer Smith, Galbraith replied, "He is incurably insane."

The Menninger psychologists described Cook as a "schizophrenic who is seriously ill."

Dr. Wechsler added, "He could not form an intention in advance to commit a crime like the Mosser killings."

But Dr. James H. Parker insisted the close-mouthed ex-convict was a "true criminal, who is feigning insanity to avoid the chair."

Dr. Waymon Thompson agreed.

Dr. Moorman Prosser, asked if he believed Cook was insane, replied, "He's crazy like a fox."

Dr. Parker said that Cook wouldn't talk to him when he visited him in his jail cell. "He obeyed his guard and seemed to understand what was said to him, but at no time during two visits did he utter a word—just went into a deep freeze."

"Does he know the difference between right and wrong and the consequences of his actions?" asked Shelton.

Dr. Parker nodded. "He showed that in the way he eluded officers for days and disposed of the Mosser bodies."

The second day of the hearing was scheduled for attorneys to make closing arguments. The hearing opened at 10:30 A.M.

Shelton asked the court, "Was this a competency hearing or a full sanity hearing? If it was a sanity hearing by the statutes, I respectfully request a continuance until next Monday when I will have seventy witnesses here.

"I will show that the defendant planned all his acts from beginning to end. I say he was able to make plans and to think and form intents as the situations demanded.

"Cook had to scheme to get the members of the Mosser family tied so he could kill them. Is that the act of a three-year-old child?

"I will show that when he kidnapped Forrest Damron and Jim Burke in Mexico, he took Burke's identification papers and the papers to his car. And he told these men that from then on he would be Jim Burke in Mexico. Is that the act of a three-year-old child?

"I want to show that he went to El Paso before he began this trail of terror and went over into Juarez and engaged in fun and frolic. He wanted to buy a Mexican girl. And the psychologists have said he has no emotions.

"He's shamming!" the district attorney insisted.

Judge Chandler said, "Mr. Shelton, of course it was a sanity hearing. I thought we all understood that. I feel at this time that this plea should stand."

Gomer Smith told Shelton, "We will admit everything you say. A plea of guilty is a complete confession to all counts in an indictment." To the court: "Now, if, as your honor has indicated, you have made up your mind, I see no point in either side orating further."

The judge began, "When the handling of this case fell to my lot, it seemed easy. This lad was in as straitened circumstances as a man can be. I appointed attorneys for him whom I consider exceptionally qualified.

"They advanced to enter a guilty plea. They say he is competent to enter a plea.

"All seven experts have said Cook knows right from wrong, which is the legal test.

"I find he has sufficient mental capacity to enter a plea, and I accept the plea.

"The question now is 'Shall we have a jury trial for the purpose of determining whether the death penalty should be imposed?'

"I have heard the statement of the psychiatrists. I have observed the defendant closely since this hearing began. It is my conclusion that there was no malice or aforethought in these crimes.

"A person must be fully chargeable with the acts he commits. The law does not contemplate malice aforethought when a person's mental capacity is doubtful. The magnitude of the crime should not be considered the same.

"I deny trial by jury. I am now and always have been a firm believer in capital punishment. Society stands indicted for allowing this child to grow up under such cruel and inhuman treatment."

At this point Chandler paused. Obviously prepared for what was to come, Shelton sprang to his feet and addressed the court in a strained voice.

"As district attorney of this federal district, I respectfully disagree with every word the court has uttered. There was malice aforethought in these crimes, and meager surroundings have no part in the consideration of this case.

"My mother died, too, when I was five. I lived in a dugout! Such a beginning does not excuse the murder of six innocent people."

Shelton railed at what he called a tendency of the federal judiciary to eliminate the jury system in favor of "one-man justice." While declaring he was making no personal attack on Judge Chandler, "I do rebel against any judge who will not give a full and complete hearing on evidence in a case.

"If ever a crime deserved the death penalty, this is it! I want the court and society and the public to know where law enforcement stands."

Judge Chandler nodded. "I understand your right to an opinion, but I am familiar with the facts in this case."

He turned to the prisoner. An expectant hush settled over the packed courtroom.

"William Edward Cook, Jr.—stand up, I sentence you to the custody of the attorney general for a period of sixty years on the first count, and for a like sentence on each of the other four counts to run consecutively. I further recommend that you be committed to Alcatraz."

The consecutive terms totaled three hundred years.

A glance at the courtroom clock showed it was 10:55 A.M. The full day scheduled for attorneys' arguments had lasted just twenty-five minutes.

Visibly brightened, Cook emerged from his stolidity and was ushered from the room. The crowd milled about, muttering. There was no demonstration. Judge Chandler had ordered deputy marshals stationed around the room to guard against any possible disturbance.

Shelton went to his office, fuming. He called the sentencing, "The damnedest travesty on justice ever!"

He pointed out that a new federal law passed in July 1950 made it possible for a prisoner to be released on parole after serving fifteen years of a life sentence or a sentence of forty-five years or more.

"In federal parlance, Cook would be eligible for parole when he is thirty-eight!"

Immediately he petitioned the attorney general to release Cook to California or Missouri, where state murder charges were pending. Within hours, the justice department in Washington announced it would honor a request by the state of California to try Cook in Imperial County for the murder of Robert Dewey, after completing his normal screening period at Alcatraz.

CHAPTER 16
THE END AT SAN QUENTIN

Judge Chandler drew bitter criticism from the public and the press. The *Tulsa Tribune* said that he should have heard all the facts and not decided Cook's fate on the conclusions of psychiatrists and that it was pinning a bit much faith in this inexact method of diagnosis.

The paper further said that Chandler indicted society in general for bringing the young man up in a vacuum. It was an unfortunate bit of characterization. The judge's observation would have been more sagacious had he said the appointed guardians of society, in this instance the courts of Missouri and their agents, had been neglectful.

The newspaper editorial went on to state that it is by no means our common practice to neglect orphans or castaways. Publicly and privately, we spend millions annually to reconstitute their home lives. Cook's adverse personality seems to have made him a shunned figure from boyhood. But he had compiled a police record before embarking on his last career of murder. If society in general had dropped him from notice, which it had reason to do, the authorities need not and should not have done so.

Another editor complained that the time for intercession of psychiatrists was when Cook was in reform school. Permanent incarceration then would have left the Mossers and Dewey alive.

And the *Tulsa World* made this scorching observation: "The judge seemed to give precedence to conditions about Joplin twenty years or more ago over the terrible facts of kidnapping and murder which touched five states. Pursuing the guilt of 'society' to the ultimate, it could be said that the mining companies of Joplin were guilty of giving Cook a diabolical opportunity because they made a hole in the ground where he was to hide his five victims."

Many heartily agreed with Chandler's decision. One citizen wrote the Oklahoma City *Times:* "The judge was on the spot in an apparent design to give this young mass killer the works in the shortest and quickest way possible. He not only was on this kind of spot with the public but was also confronted by a prosecutor who had subpoenaed some 73 witnesses. In the face of all this the judge retained his deep sense of responsibility to recognize and protect the legal rights of each individual who comes before him regardless of who that individual may be . . . The public needs more judges who will recognize and resolutely protect the rights of the individual citizen whether it involves his life, property or his liberty." But the following letter expressed the more general view:

Editor of the *Times:*
So society takes the rap? It's society's fault that Bill Cook killed six unarmed, defenseless people!
That being the case, why not spring Cook and let society stand trial? On the face of it, perhaps that's already happened.
So Cook was "incapable" of exercising "intent" in the Mosser murders? Guess the poor unfortunate picked up that gun in El Paso as a plaything. . .
A tip of the new spring bonnet to District Attorney Shelton for sticking to his guns, and to the U.S. attorney general for backing him up.
Now, let's sit back and see how California desert justice reacts to murder.

Cook left Oklahoma City on Saturday night, March 24, in the custody of U.S. Marshal Rex Hawks and two deputies. He wore handcuffs, leg irons and a chain passed from the seat about his middle, like an airplane safety belt.

When he stepped off the train at Emeryville, California, two days later, he still had heavy chains on his wrists. His face was expressionless as he was driven across the bay to the San Francisco municipal pier, where Warden Edwin Swope and other Alcatraz officials awaited him.

"We'll treat him just like the rest of them," said the warden.

Cook was hustled aboard the prison boat, the gang-plank was raised and soon he was on his way to begin the longest sentence ever carried to America's tough-boy prison.

His parting shot to Marshal Hawks: "If the California law waits to get me, I'll be a little too old to serve any more time."

But the wheels of California justice were already spinning in high gear. District Attorney Don Bitler obtained one of the speediest indictments in Imperial County history. In Washington, Attorney General J. Howard McGrath reviewed psychiatric reports furnished by James V. Bennett, director of the Bureau of Prisons, declaring Cook sane, and announced he would stand trial in Imperial County. Cook was removed to El Centro under guard of four deputy marshals and a special custodial officer from Alcatraz.

Arraigned before Superior Court Judge Luray J. Mouser on October 13, the stocky killer stood tight-lipped and sullen and refused to answer even the question: "What is your name?"

He sent a telegram to the court-appointed attorneys in his federal kidnapping trial asking if they could defend him.

Connolly flew to El Centro.

Again Connolly raised the question of his client's mental capacity. "He hasn't changed," Connolly told the court. "I talked with him three hours, and he showed great indifference to his case. The whole thing apparently doesn't mean anything to him."

He entered a double plea for Cook—not guilty and not guilty by reason of insanity. (Under a peculiarity of the California legal code, Cook would first be tried on his simple plea of not guilty to Dewey's murder. If convicted, he would then have a chance to prove himself insane.)

At the same time, Connolly asked Judge Mouser for a stay of proceedings pending an examination of Cook by alienists. "Four psychiatrists, in his first trial, reported him insane."

Judge Mouser ruled that such a request should be accompanied by affidavits from the psychiatrists. Connolly withdrew his motion. "We also withdraw the not guilty plea," he said. "The second part of the plea, 'not guilty by reason of insanity,' stands."

Cook's innocence or guilt would now have no bearing on the hearing. As Connolly told reporters later, "Actually, all it does is relieve the state of proving the crime from a technical standpoint. The jury will decide only one question—Cook's mental condition at the time Dewey was slain. If the jury finds him sane, the judge will decide the 'degree of murder' and pronounce sentence. If he finds him insane, he will be returned to his cell at Alcatraz."

Judge Mouser set the trial for November 19 and appointed three psychiatrists of state mental institutions—Dr. Thomas Haggarty of Stockton, Dr. O. L. Gierke of Camarillo and Dr. F. H. Garrett of Patton State Hospital—to examine the prisoner.

Connolly disclosed that Dr. Hugh Galbraith of Oklahoma City would testify for the defense. He also called Mrs. Bernie Goff Bryson, former Joplin probation officer, and Dr. Frederick Hacker, noted Beverly Hills, California, psychiatrist, as witnesses.

Spectators packed the courtroom as the trial began. The front row of seats was roped off as a security measure. Seated directly in front of the roped-off section were Alcatraz prison officials. Deputy marshals flanked Cook on either side and five feet to the rear. An Imperial County deputy sheriff guarded each door.

Cook sat solidly in his chair, feet planted firmly on the floor. His elbows never moved from the arms of the chair and he kept his eyes averted, staring at the floor in front of him.

As required when the issue of insanity is pleaded under California law, the defense presented its case first. Connolly called Mrs. Bryson as the first witness.

She described the sordid conditions of Cook's cave-like home life and the death of his mother. "He had the worst inferiority complex of any boy I ever dealt with, and finding his mother's dead body with blows all over her face was a shock that he could never forget.

"I am no psychiatrist," Mrs. Bryson told the jury, "but I don't believe anyone in his right mind could commit the crimes Bill did."

In reply to a question, "Did you ever attempt to have Cook examined for insanity?" by Charles F. Sturdivant, deputy district prosecutor, Mrs. Bryson looked down and said, "Unfortunately, no."

Galbraith again testified to Cook's "very disorganized mind," his "difficulty in emotional expression, in thinking and dealing with people."

"On January 6, did this boy have capacity to entertain malice aforethought?" Connolly asked.

"None whatever," Galbraith answered. "Everything he does is without deliberation. He reacts automatically."

He further described Cook as "not the type of person we hold responsible in mental hospitals."

He added: "We take great pains to protect other people from them."

Sturdivant questioned the doctor at length about "awareness of the consequences" of murder on the day Dewey was slain. "Does Cook know the difference between right and wrong, and did he know the difference on January 6? Was he aware he had shot a man?"

"He never gave it a thought afterward," Galbraith replied.

Pressed about Cook's ability to tell right from wrong, the doctor answered: "Anybody knows right from wrong unless he is unconscious. Mentally ill people know the difference but fail to carry their knowledge into actions. Actions are important in mental illnesses, not what a person may say to you."

Finally, Judge Mouser turned to Galbraith and asked him if he thought Cook was insane—a word the psychiatrist dodged throughout the testimony—and the doctor's reply was sharp and almost angry. "He is one of the most insane men I ever met," he said, and left the courtroom immediately when excused from the witness stand.

Dr. Frederick Hacker described Cook as "suffering from schizophrenia.

"His thinking processes are not good. He knows who he is; he knows where he is and he can give a fairly rational account of all that has happened to him.

"But he is incapable of establishing a connection between a reason for an act and an act itself. He is completely impassive. Nothing elicits any emotion from him. He is aware of his danger, but it doesn't affect him in any way.

"He refers to actual killings without any emotion. He has never entertained a thought about the feelings of the relatives and loved ones of those he killed—he falls asleep when he tries."

Dr. Hacker spoke with a great deal of animation and gesture as he labored and paused frequently searching for words to express himself "without being too technical." He had a heavy Austrian accent, but spoke precisely.

Opening the case for the prosecution, Deputy Sheriff Homer Waldrip related how he had been kidnapped by Cook. "He told me about killing the Mossers a few days earlier, and said he would have to kill me too." He described Cook as "fully rational."

Damron and Burke told how Cook had steered them all over Baja California for seven days—with a gun in their backs. He was "the complete boss" and "calm, cool and deliberate."

The state psychiatrists agreed that Cook was a "psychopathic type of person, but there is no evidence of insanity."

Questioning Dr. Giercke, Connolly turned suddenly and pointed to the stoic 23-year-old killer staring at the floor.

"Do you mean to say you think this boy is faking?" Connolly asked.

"Faking what?" the doctor answered. "He isn't doing anything but remaining immobile."

The key testimony came from FBI Agent Henry Plaxico, who had taken Cook's confession. "After admitting the murders of the Mosser family and Dewey, he told me, 'The only thing to do now is to act crazy and get the sympathy of the people.'"

Connolly jumped to his feet and asked the agent if he meant "to tell this jury that this boy told you he was going to *act* crazy?"

"I've already told them that," Plaxico replied calmly.

Sturdivant and Connolly presented the closing arguments. Sturdivant pointed to what he believed were the "positive facts"—that Cook was sane at the time he shot and killed Robert Dewey; that he planned all his moves, knew the consequences of the act, changed shirts to conceal his identity, routed his trip to Mexico to avoid the law and disposed of the license plates on Dewey's car because he knew the officers would be looking for them.

"Three alienists have found him to be a sane man—a desperate man, to be sure, but a sane man. But once caught," the deputy prosecutor emphasized, "he decided the best thing to do was act crazy and get the sympathy of the people."

Connolly then launched an attack against the methods used by the prosecution before the trial and the substance of the state's testimony. He denounced "the act of bringing three alienists employed by the state to examine the defendant and then calling in witnesses to try the defendant in a rump, or kangaroo court." He rapped the testimony of Drs. Haggarty, Giercke and Garrett, "all superintendents of California state mental institutions—administrators, who are psychiatrists in name only." Then he lashed out at District Attorney Don Bitler, declaring him "a very ambitious man who wanted to try this case to advance his ambitions.

"When he heard criticism in the county that getting Cook down here from Alcatraz would cost a lot of money, he went before civic clubs and got his stooges to do the same to give the history of the case. Not content with a Roman holiday, Bitler then went on the air to whip up feeling against this boy.

"He told the people the boy would be out of Alcatraz in fifteen years, when we know in Oklahoma City the federal judge sentenced him to five sixty-year terms to run consecutively, not concurrently, for the very purpose of keeping him behind bars the rest of his life.

"I say, 'Shame on you, Don Bitler!'" Connolly cried. "I like to see ambition, but I can't stand to see it realized by the blood of a human being.

"I don't attempt to minimize, and I'm sure no one wants to minimize the horror of this boy's deeds. But there is no point in taking the life of an insane man."

With a plea for justice based on consideration of partial evidence, Connolly ended his argument.

Bitler himself made the closing remarks: "Years ago, the eminent lawyer Clarence Darrow, giving advice to a young attorney, said, 'If the facts are on your side, argue the facts; if the law is on your side, argue the law; if you have neither the facts nor the law on your side, attack the district attorney.'

"Mr. Connolly has devoted seventeen minutes of his thirty-five-minute summation to attacking me as district attorney."

It took the jury of eight women and four men just fifty minutes to find Bill Cook sane.

The quick verdict caught everyone by surprise. It was necessary to return Cook from the county jail, and the jury had to wait fifteen minutes until the lawyers could be called to court.

When the verdict was read, Cook sat rock still—as he had throughout the trial; his guards watched for any untoward movement. There was none. He literally failed to bat an eye.

Judge Mouser asked Connolly if he wished the jury polled.

The obviously dejected attorney answered, "I don't believe so."

He immediately served notice of appeal to the California supreme court. It wasn't necessary. California law provides for an automatic review of a case by the higher court where the death penalty is imposed.

Mouser then asked the attorneys to present evidence to determine the "degree of murder." Rather than have further witnesses called, they agreed that the judge could reach his decision on the testimony of witnesses in the sanity hearing, testimony of witnesses before the Imperial County grand jury which indicted Cook, and FBI reports.

The principal FBI report turned over to Mouser was that of ballistics expert R. M. Zimmers.

Before accepting the lawyers' agreement on the "no further testimony" procedure, the judge asked Cook if the arrangements were agreeable.

Cook glanced toward the bench, then turned to Connolly. Connolly whispered briefly to his client. Then Cook replied to Judge Mouser with the only word he had yet spoken in court. It was a barely audible "Yes."

On November 27, Judge Mouser ruled Dewey's killing "willful, deliberate and premeditated—committed in perpetration of a felony, robbery." He scheduled formal sentencing for 2 P.M. the day following.

Again spectators packed the courtroom. The judge asked Bitler and Connolly for comment.

Bitler said: "In my forty years as a reporter, defender prosecutor, I've never seen a murder case that fit California's definition of first degree murder so well.

"Justice means in simple words to give a man that which he deserves. We believe the interests of justice demand that William Edward Cook forfeit his right to live in a society which he has so maliciously offended."

Connolly's only comment was to ask the court to strike Bitler's remarks from the record. Judge Mouser denied the request and added that the district attorney's remarks had no influence on his judgment.

"I've already made up my mind," he said.

Cook stood with head lowered, his face unmoved. He did, however, make care of his few statements. He said, "No," when

Judge Mouser asked if there was any reason why he should not pronounce the sentence.

The judge stated he was aware that Cook was "emotionally unstable but pointed out that he had admitted the murder of Dewey, had been found sane by a jury, and that the degree of murder had been found to be the first degree."

When he completed the charge and said, "I sentence you to death," Cook paled slightly. A few seconds later a half-smirk appeared on his thick lips.

Three guards virtually pounced on the badman. He was handcuffed to the county jailer and hustled back to his cell. Inside the court railing, nine heavily armed sheriff's deputies were stationed at vantage points, including several unbarred windows, to prevent any attempt to escape.

Handcuffed and shackled to two Imperial County deputy sheriffs, doomed Billy Cook left Imperial Valley for the last time before dawn Saturday, December 1, en route to San Quentin prison. On May 7, 1952, Attorney John Connolly made his last appeal for Cook's life. He told the California supreme court it should commute the Missouri killer's death sentence to life imprisonment because he was "obviously insane." District Attorney Bitler contended the question of sanity "had been fairly determined by a jury." The supreme court unanimously confirmed the jury verdict.

The court's order went down to Trial Judge Mouser. Mouser set Cook's execution date for December 12.

During the last full day of his life, December 11, Cook sat moodily on his prison cot in death row reading newspapers and listening to the radio. He refused to accept the comfort of the prison chaplain or talk with Warden Harly O. Teets or newsmen.

His only show of interest was in the menu for his last meal. Cook ordered fried chicken, french fried potatoes, peas, pumpkin pie, coffee and milk.

Sullen and defiant to the last, the youth entered the prison's green-walled gas chamber flanked by two guards with one guard bringing up the rear. He was helped into the chamber's heavy wooden execution chair, and while being strapped in, looked around the eight-sided room as if completely oblivious to the presence of some fifty witnesses.

When the chamber's door closed at 10:03 A.M. and the lethal

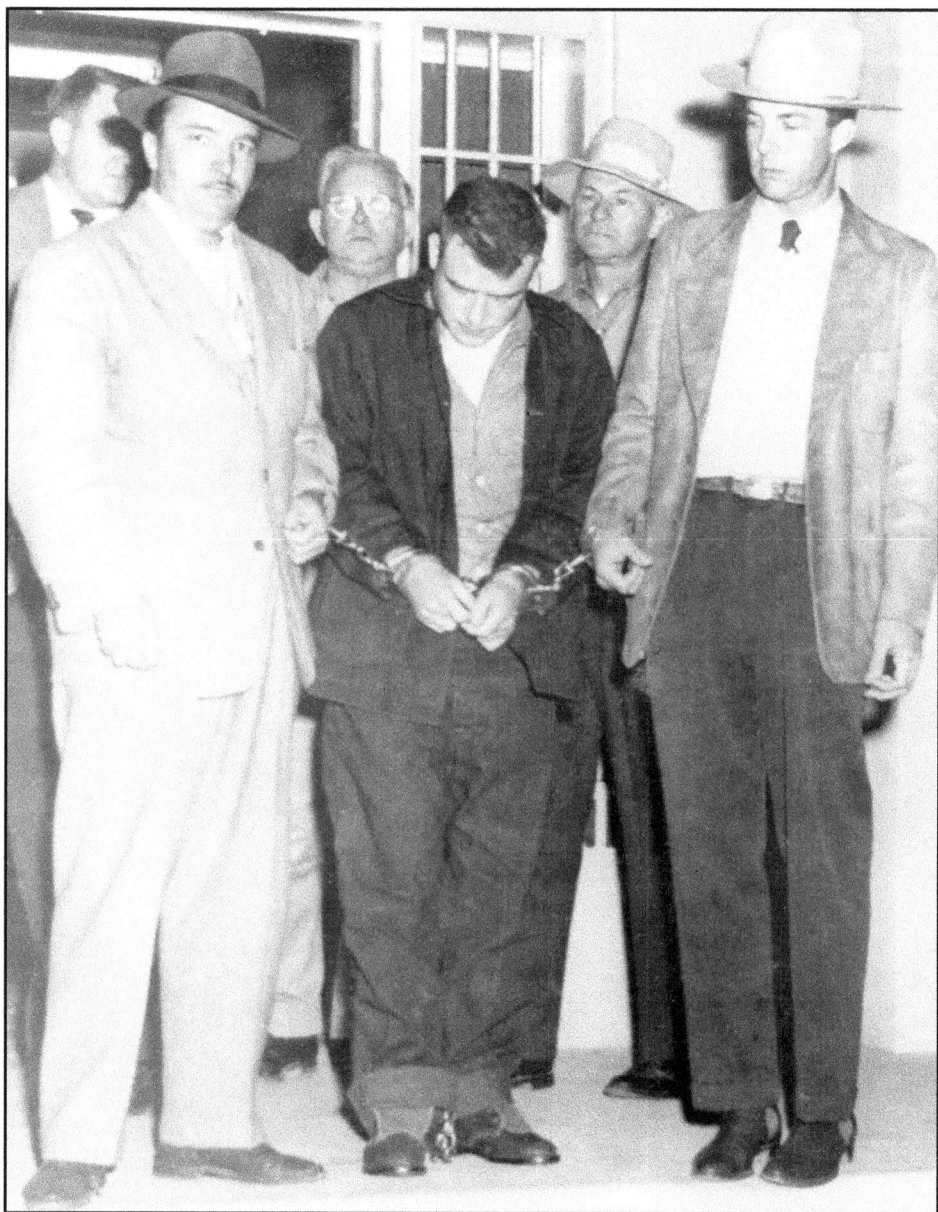

Cook's last ride en route to San Quentin prior to his execution for the murder of Robert Dewey. (L to r) Deputy Sheriff Wes Minor; Deputy U.S. Marshal Ray Walgren; official wearing glasses, unidentified; Cook, in handcuffs and leg irons; Lieutenant E. E. Ryckner of the Alcatraz custodial corps; Bob Jensen, Chief Criminal Deputy, Imperial County, California.

cyanide pellets were dropped, Cook's hands clenched. As the fumes began to fill the room, his hands remained closed and the word "HARD" across his fingers was clearly visible.

He held back his head, inhaling the fumes. He did not struggle against death. The audible signs of his dying were three distinct gasps.

Live by the gun and roam was his credo. He would roam no more.

EPILOGUE

The Hitch-Hiker

As an aftermath of the Mosser family tragedy, the daily gesture of giving a man a lift in bad weather, hardship cases, or just to have his company, came to a cautious halt. The tragedy provoked a demand for anti-hitchhiker laws nationwide.

In Oklahoma, a bill was introduced in the house of representatives, making it a misdemeanor to solicit a ride from the right-of-way of any state or federal highway, exempting persons seeking transportation from regularly licensed motor carriers at regularly designated points of embarkation or debarkation. Other state legislatures put more teeth into existing statutes, with no exemptions whatever. One state adopted a law requiring that hitchhikers carry identification cards which must be presented for a driver's inspection, and posted signs warning motorists that they take such persons into their cars at a deadly risk. City councils in turn were pressured to consider ordinances making it a misdemeanor to hitchhike in the city limits or for motorists to pick them up. Newspapers conducted random interviews, publishing reactions and answers to the question: "What would you have done in Carl Mosser's shoes?"

Cook's orgy of violence also stirred interest of the motion picture industry. In California, producer Collier Young, of Filmmakers Productions, and Ida Lupino, who had established herself as Hollywood's leading woman director as well as one of its better actresses, found the segment of Cook's flight into Baja, Mexico, more urgent than fiction. "The deeper we delved into the subject," they reported later, "the more excited we became. We were dealing with

Advertising sheets for The Hitch-Hiker, starring Edmond O'Brien, Frank Lovejoy, and William Talman (Filmmakers Production, distributed by RKO Radio Pictures, 1953).

real people caught in one of the most dramatic adventures of our times. The basic theme was the question—in a race against death—which survives? The sane or the criminal mind?" Their answer was an off-beat, driving suspense drama, distributed by RKO Radio Pictures in 1953, entitled *The Hitch-Hiker.*

In addition to directing *The Hitch-Hiker,* Lupino wrote the screenplay in collaboration with producer Young and obtained a superlative acting cast topped by Edmond O'Brien and Frank Lovejoy, as the captives; William Talman, in the role of the droopy-eyed highway killer; and Joe Torvay as the pursuing Mexican police chief called Captain Alvarado.

A woman director was nothing new to the two husky stars, O'Brien and Lovejoy. O'Brien had appeared on Broadway under the direction of Margaret Webster and the late Auriol Lee while Lovejoy credited the late Antoinette Perry with teaching him much of what he knew about acting when he starred in Miss Perry's staged *Chalked Out.* O'Brien boasted a distinguished career as a Shakespearean actor in New York. He was Mercuito in Laurence Olivier and Vivien Leigh's production of *Romeo and Juliet,* and had appeared with John Gielgud in *Hamlet,* with Maurice Evans in *Henry IV,* and with Orson Welles in *Julius Caesar.* He also had scored well in his Hollywood debut, *The Hunchback of Notre Dame.*

William Talman, whose star had been rising steadily with his portrayals of the honest young cop in *The Racket* and the Air Force colonel in *One Minute to Zero,* loved to act tough and welcomed the complete change of pace when offered the role of the highway death-dealer. He was warned that it would be physically difficult to play. Nevertheless, each morning he painfully donned a rubber piece glued over his right eyelid with liquid adhesive, which gave him the appearance of a paralyzed eye that never closed. "It just about drove me crazy," he admitted, "but I grinned and bore it."

Jose Torvay, a prominent Mexican character actor, had appeared in more than 400 pictures. He had starred in the first talking picture made in Mexico, and made his Hollywood debut in *The Treasure of the Sierra Madre.*

O'Brien and Lovejoy are completely believable as two peace-loving Americans on a fishing expedition in Mexico, who pick up a stranger stranded on the highway only to discover that their passenger is a maniacal murderer attempting to escape the law in a mad

Devil with a thumb. Here William Talman portrays the ride-thumbing murderer in The Hitch-Hiker *(1953).*

Droopy-eyed William Talman keeps revolver trained on his captives even while he catnaps. Scene from The Hitch-Hiker *(1953).*

Droopy-eyed William Talman (standing, center) holds Edmond O'Brien and Frank Lovejoy hostages. Suspense mounts as they try to outwit Talman before reaching the Mexican gulf port where Talman intends to kill them and escape to Central America. Scene from The Hitch-Hiker (1953).

dash across the rugged Mexican terrain to a gulf port from which he hopes to escape to Central America. Their journey—paralleling in many aspects the manhunt headlined in newspapers less than two years before—is fraught with terror as they try to outwit their captor while constantly at gunpoint, knowing that he plans to kill them when they reach his destination. Suspense and emotion never slacken as they proceed on their weird journey to a climax that would make any audience hold its breath.

The Trade Press classed *The Hitch-Hiker* "among the best in the suspense melodrama division" and praised co-stars O'Brien, Lovejoy and Talman as "Oscar candidates." Theater owners enlisted the cooperation of local newspapers and merchants in offering prizes and passes for the best 150-word letters on "My Experience With a Hitch-Hiker." The movie lent itself to powerful editorials warning motorists against the risk of picking up road riders, citing numerous instances where robbery, violence, and even murder had resulted. Local safety councils cooperated in the campaign by displaying "Beware of the Hitch-Hiker" posters on streetcars, buses and other places of vantage. Police departments endorsed "Be Careful of the Hitch-Hiker" stencils of a large hand with thumb upraised on sidewalks at major intersections. And prizes were offered for the best last line to the following Safety Jingle:

> Though a hitch-hiker's thumb up ahead
> Doesn't fill you with ominous dread
> Don't pull alongside to offer a ride
> _____
>
> (Sample lines)
> Or you may face a gun full of lead!
> Better gun up your motor instead:
> Be careful: You may wind up dead!

All in all, the nation experienced a rude awakening, and the millions who witnessed *The Hitch-Hiker* on screen remembered its seventy minutes for a long, long time.

BIBLIOGRAPHY

DOCUMENTARY

Author's personal knowledge of the Cook case; numerous interviews and conversations with local, state, and federal law enforcement officers who participated in the manhunt; and statements of witnesses and persons who knew Cook before he became the nation's most wanted fugitive.

Extensive interview of March 25, 1951, with United States Attorney Robert E. Shelton, of Oklahoma City, Oklahoma, who prosecuted William Edward Cook, Jr. under the Lindbergh Kidnap Act of 1932, which, as later amended, provided the death penalty for transporting a kidnapped person across a state line.

NEWSPAPERS
Original news reports:

Daily Oklahoman, January 4–9, 11–12, 15–19, 21–23, and 25, 1951; February 20, 1951; March 1, 13–14, 19–24, 1951; April 13 and 22, 1951; June 2, 1951; August 22, 1951; September 20, 1951; October 6–7, 10, 13–14, 1951; November 17, 19–25, 28–29, 1951; December 1, 1951; August 27, 1952; October 10, 1952; December 7, 10, 16–19, and 21, 1952.
Imperial Valley Press (El Centro, Calif.), October 8–12, 16, 19–29, 1951; December 12, 1952.
Oklahoma City Times, January 4–10, 12–13, 16–19, 22 and 25, 1951; February 20 and 23, 1951; March 1, 22–24 and 27, 1951;

October 13, 1951; November 22–24 and 29, 1951; December 15 and 17, 1952.

The Post Press (El Centro, Calif.), October 7, 14 and 21, 1951; November 25, 1951; December 2, 1951.

St. Louis Post-Dispatch, January 21, 1951.

Tulsa Daily World, January 4–19, 21 and 23, 1951; March 21 and 25, 1951; April 14, 1951; October 6 and 12, 1951, November 20–22, 28–29, 1951; May 9, 1952; September 19 and 26, 1952; December 3, 13 and 15, 1952; September 12, 1963.

Tulsa Tribune, January 4–6, 9–13, 17 and 25, 1951; March 1, 1951; April 14, 1951.

Wichita Falls (Texas) Times, January 5–6, 1951.

Associated Press and *United Press* dispatches:

ATWOOD, Ill., Jan. 18 (*Tulsa Daily World*, January 1, 1951).

BLYTHE, Calif., Jan. 6 (*Tulsa Daily World*, January 7, 1951).

COMANCHE, Okla., Dec. 14 (*Tulsa Daily World*, December 15, 1951).

———, Dec. 15 (*Oklahoma City Times*, December 15, 1951).

EL CENTRO Calif., Jan. 8 (*Tulsa Daily World*, January 9, 1951) .

———, Jan. 9 (*Tulsa Daily World*, January 10, 1951).

———, Jan. 11 (*Tulsa Tribune*, January 11, 1951).

———, Jan. 12 (*Tulsa Tribune*, January 12, 1951).

———, March 22 (*Tulsa Tribune*, March 22, 1951).

———, Aug. 21 (*Daily Oklahoman*, August 22, 1951).

———, Sept. 19 (*Daily Oklahoman*, September 20, 1951).

———, Oct. 5 (*Tulsa Daily World*, October 6, 1951).

———, Oct. 6 (*Daily Oklahoman*, October 7, 1951).

———, Oct. 11 (*Tulsa Daily World*, October 12,1951).

———, Oct. 13 (*Daily Oklahoman*, October 14, 1951).

———, Nov. 18 (*Daily Oklahoman*, November 1, 1951).

———, Nov. 19 (*Daily Oklahoman*, November 20, 1951, and *Tulsa Daily World*, November 20, 1951).

———, Nov. 20 (*Daily Oklahoman*, November 21, 1951, and *Tulsa Daily World*, November 22, 1951).

———, Nov. 22 (*Oklahoma City Times*, November 22, 1951, and *Tulsa Daily World*, November 23, 1951).

———, Nov. 23 (*Oklahoma City Times*, November 23, 1951, and *Daily Oklahoman*, November 24, 1951).

———, Nov. 24 (*Oklahoma City Times*, November 24, 1951, and *Daily Oklahoman*, November 25, 1951).

———, Nov. 27 (*Daily Oklahoman*, November 28, 1951 and *Tulsa Daily World*, November 28, 1951).

———, Nov. 28 (*Daily Oklahoman*, November 29, 1951, and *Tulsa Daily World*, November 29, 1951).

———, Nov. 29 (*Daily Oklahoman*, November 29, 1951).

HAMMOND, Ill., Jan 24 (*Daily Oklahoman*, January 25, 1951).

JOPLIN, Mo., Jan. 12 (*Tulsa Daily World*, January 13, 1951).

———, Jan. 19 (*Oklahoma City Times*, January 19, 1951).

SAN FRANCISCO, Calif., May 7 (*Tulsa Daily World*, May 8, 1952).

———, Sept. 25 (*Tulsa Daily World*, September 26, 1952).

SAN DIEGO, Calif., Jan. 7 (*Tulsa Daily World*, January 8, 1951).

———, Jan. 9 (*Tulsa Tribune*, January 9, 1951).

———, Jan. 18 (*Tulsa Daily World*, January 19, 1951).

———, Jan. 19 (*Oklahoma City Times*, January 19, 1951).

SAN QUENTIN, Calif., Dec. 12 (*Oklahoma City Times*, December 12, 1952, and *Tulsa Daily World*, December 13, 1952).

Editorials and pictorial features:

"Behind the Scenes in FBI Manhunt," *Daily Oklahoman*, January 21, 1951.

"The Cook–Mosser Story," *Daily Oklahoman*, March 25, 1951.

"Cook to Die—We to Learn," *Tulsa Tribune*, March 22, 1951.

"Do We Need State Police?" *Tulsa Tribune*, January 11, 1951.

"Here's Trail of Terror Blazed Through West," *Oklahoma City Times*, January 16, 1951.

"Most Amazing Desperado," *Tulsa Daily World*, March 21, 1951.

"Scenes from Cook Capture, Recovery of Mosser Bodies; Key Figures in Case," *Tulsa Daily World*, January 16, 1951.

"Stiff Reaction in Cook Base," *Tulsa Daily World*, March 23, 1951.

"Where the Public Can Help," *Daily Oklahoman*, January 12, 1951.

BOOKS

Nash, J. Robert. *Bloodletters and Badmen, A Narrative Encyclopedia of American Criminals from the Pilgrims to the Present.* New York: M. Evans and Company, Inc., 1973. (Entry pages 129–132: "Cook, William. Murderer, Robber, 1929–1952.)

Shirley, Glenn. *Born to Kill, He Blazed A Trail of Death and Terror Across Fourteen States.* Derby, Connecticut: Monarch Books, Inc., 1963. (Copyright renewed by author, 1991.)

Sifakis, Carl. *The Encyclopedia of American Crimes.* New York: Smithmark Publishers, Inc., 1982. (Entry pages 170–171: "Cook, William. Mass murderer, 1929–1952.")

ARTICLES

Asher, Gilbert. "Cook's Crime Career 23 Years in Making." *Tulsa Daily World*, January 21, 1951.

Bulloch, Nolen. "Put Yourself in Carl Mosser's Place." *Tulsa Tribune*, January 25, 1951.

Conley, Claire. "Crowds at Bill Cook's Coffin Baffle City Psychiatrists." *Oklahoma City Times*, December 17, 1952.

Etheridge, Charles. "300 Years Could Boil Down to Only 20 for Killer Cook," *Daily Oklahoman*, April 22, 1951.

Glynn, Dean (pseudonym of Glenn Shirley). "Born to Kill." *Saga, The Magazine for Men*, Vol. 21, No. 3, December 1960.

Hirsch, Richard. "Death on Highway 66." *True Detective*, August 1951.

Kelly, Bill. "'BadEye' Cook, The Natural Killer." *Startling Detective*, Vol. 84, No. 2, March 1994.

Swain, Paul. "If You Were In His Spot." *Daily Oklahoman*, January 21, 1951.

Taylor, Nelson J. "Cook Still Kicks Back at Life." *Daily Oklahoman*, January 10, 1951.

Wyden, Peter. "Case History of a Badman." *St. Louis Post Dispatch*, January 21, 1951.

INDEX

www.ingramcontent.com/pod-product-compliance
Lightning Source LLC
Chambersburg PA
CBHW060054100426
42742CB00014B/2822